matisse

Sandra Orienti

Hamlyn

London   New York   Sydney   Toronto

twentieth-century masters
General editors: H. L. Jaffé and A. Busignani

© Copyright in the text by Sadea/Sansoni, Florence 1971
© Copyright in the illustrations by SPADEM, Paris 1971
© Copyright this translation The Hamlyn Publishing Group Limited 1972
London · New York · Sydney · Toronto
Hamlyn House, Feltham, Middlesex, England.
ISBN 0 600 35928 X

Colour lithography by Zincotipia Moderna, Florence
Printed in Italy by Industria Grafica L'Impronta, Scandicci, Florence
Bound in Italy by Poligrafici il Resto del Carlino, Bologna
Photo-typeset by Photoprint Plates, Rayleigh, Essex

Distributed in the United States of America by Crown Publishers Inc.

contents

List of colour plates

List of black-and-white illustrations

Green does not mean grass

'When I paint green, it doesn't mean grass; when I paint blue, it doesn't mean sky.' This is not Matisse justifying himself, it is Matisse setting down the poetic ideas that free his style from everything that is not pictorial, and that lead us on to his other important and famous statement: 'It is through colour that I am.'

Matisse's whole body of work, from the time when quite suddenly he felt called to examine himself and the meaning of his painting, until in his maturity he burst out into colour and achieved a harmonious realisation of his style and methods, seems to be found in those words. In them lies everything that cannot be explained and cannot be precisely defined about his use of colour: in other words, about his painting. Matisse's painting moves in a kind of classical way, gradually manifesting a logic of its own in spite of the overwhelming use of colour. There is no theorising at the time, no statement of intent. Words may be used later on, to clarify things in himself and in his art.

Everything develops within the painting itself, indeed within the maze Matisse himself is examining. From this, there is only one way out, but even Matisse himself cannot always see it. Whenever he paints he puts the whole of himself into it, all his experience and knowledge; yet once more, he invents all the possibilities that exist in painting; and each time he knows for certain that he will be radically challenging his own values, his own life.

Matisse's whole artistic activity covers painting, sculpture, graphics, and *gouaches decoupées*, yet the temptation is always to concentrate on his short Fauve period, during which he painted so intensely, and to compare this period with the rest of his work and with other art movements of the same period, Cubism in particular. The Fauve period was certainly a critically important time for Matisse, a time in which currents and movements were divided. On the other hand, when he said that he would 'permit' Cubism, it did not mean that he felt superior, contemptuous and condescending towards it, but that he felt outside it. It was one of the most influential movements in twentieth-century art, but he felt he could not be directly involved with it.

This saying, 'green—that doesn't mean grass', lies at the root of all Matisse's painting. It means that by a glowing, purified use of colour he got away entirely from the claims of nature and achieved a unity of composition in his painting, not through the ordered use of perspective, but through a kind of hierarchical arrangement of space and colour. So it was not the representation of reality that attracted him to his subject, but the tensions involved in it.

It is not, in fact, a case of 'representation' at all. The picture itself, its own inner, yet obvious, structure, is the object of the whole exercise, and the search for colour has a double purpose: it shows both the nature of the object and the space in which it is found.

Maurice Denis maintained that a painting was mainly 'a surface covered in colours arranged in a certain order'; and it was Gauguin who took this a step further by arranging the zones of colour in such a way that the spatial plane was shown and built up, though not generated in any autonomous way. Of Gauguin, Matisse spoke little, yet his influence can be seen in Matisse's painting, or at least, as Estienne put it, there are 'hints of a pictorial atmosphere that is clearly the responsibility of the painter of Annah the Javanese'.

Matisse's artistic personality was established during the short flowering of the Fauve group, which was never a homogeneous body. Once its years of activity were over. Matisse was the only one of its members to deepen the quality of his own painting in the light of the ideas he had developed during those years, as if he still meant to reassert what had been said in the Salon d'Automne of 1905. And in the years before 1905, his own ideas had developed, and the influences upon him had grown; he had struggled against some of these influences, and gone further than the lessons taught by Cézanne in trying to give colour as important a function in the structure as the volumes and spaces.

This is why the years before 1905 are much more important than they might at first appear, in their effect upon Matisse's later work. They are important not so much for the influences that determined how it was to develop, as for the fact that they reflected the special atmosphere of art and culture around the end of the last century and the beginning of this one, and revealed all the unresolved contradictions of the time.

It is by analysing the original influences upon Matisse that one comes to realise how, although leader of the Fauves, he was very much himself, a single figure who was not to be reduced and circumscribed by the limitations of a particular movement, but who was always consistent, logical and clearly faithful to himself. Indeed, as Longhi puts it, he was the only one of the group whose 'huge parabola' of experience kept 'closely faithful to the Fauve instinct of the first decade of the century and is its most important artistic result'.

Throughout his life Matisse maintained unspoiled the quality inherent in his work. This quality speaks for itself, far better than anything which has been said or argued about it, or even maintained by Matisse himself, who said a good deal about his own work. 'The artist,' he wrote, 'puts the best of himself into his paintings. There are some who may not find it enough, but the fact remains that the artist's words do not matter in any essential way.'

The slow patient years

The years between 1890 and 1903 were those which Lassaigne called the 'slow, patient' years, that is, the time in which Matisse was seeking himself, trying to identify himself in painting.

It seems hard to believe that such an artist came into the world by chance, but the events of Matisse's life seem to support the idea.

He was born in northern France, at Le Cateau-Cambrésis, in 1869, and sent by his family to study law. Nothing seemed to suggest that he had any vocation for painting until, quite suddenly, when his mother gave him a paintbox during his convalescence after an operation in about 1890, the idea seemed to come to him. It seems an extraordinary mixture of coincidence and predestination.

Matisse gave up his job in a lawyer's office and, not without opposition, went to Paris. There he found schools and studios, masters and youthful friends. But even before he left Le Cateau-Cambrésis he had taken a course in drawing at the Ecole Quentin de la Tour, and in 1890 had painted the first two works he recognised as the beginning of his serious painting. They were both still-lifes (Daric collection, Paris), patient reflections of familiar objects, steeped in memories of seventeenth-century painting.

In Paris he attended the Académie Julian and evening classes at the Ecole des Arts Décoratifs in 1892, where he met Albert Marquet, a serious, silent man six years his junior, whose friendship was to stand up to many trials.

Then, once again, chance played an important part in his life. One day, as he was painting in the courtyard of the Ecole des Beaux-Arts, he was seen by Gustave Moreau, who was impressed with his work and got him into the school in his own famous atelier in 1895, allowing him in without the entrance examination.

At that time, Moreau's prestige at the Ecole stood high. His best gift as a teacher was a capacity to see what his pupils were worth, to make them aware of themselves and their own talents. His teaching was broadly based and liberal, never restrictive, and noticeably unacademic. Although he made his pupils study the antique and visit museums, he also insisted that they should observe everyday life, and what was going on in the street. All this meant that Moreau was fervently loved by his pupils who, as Roger-Marx put it, learnt 'to develop their own individuality'; it was also Moreau's way of being a bridge over which his pupils would pass – which indeed was what he hoped to be.

He was generous, eccentric, intellectually curious and eclectic in his taste, combining enthusiasms for Mantegna and Raphael, Chassériau and Delacroix, and managing to steep the whole in decadent symbolism, touches of Surrealism and what Huysmans called a 'learned hysteria'. All this did not prevent him from saying quite clearly and logically, however, that 'the most elementary thing in art is the method used, and the best reveals the artist's sensibility'.

In teaching Matisse, Moreau tactfully allowed him plenty of freedom, letting him make his own discoveries, inviting him to love arabesques and to find 'knowledge in the rhythm and curve of the line', and revealing to him mysterious and wonderful aspects of what was exotic in the world.

The atelier of Gustave Moreau (private collection, Paris), which Matisse painted in 1895, cannot be seen as mere homage to his master. It is more an effort to apply his clumsy, contrived use of space to the uncertain greys and browns spread slackly over the canvas, while in the foreground the model's upstanding figure, glimmering metallically, seems to be trying to enter one of Moreau's own canvases.

This slow, patient timidity also appears in the careful copies Matisse made at the Louvre: of the Dutch painters, of Poussin, of Chardin. These show him carefully exercising eye and hand, and concentrating methodically, rather than making any significant choice. The paintings in the end are respectfully accurate. So are the paintings he made in Moreau's atelier, which are suffused with shadows, or the landscapes in Brittany, painted in the summer of 1895, which show him as 'understanding the art of greyness'.

The summer of 1896, however, during which he stayed in Brittany again, at Belle-Ile, was more positive and promising. His constant dedication to painting, the familiarity of the places around him, the company of his friend Emile Wéry who in Paris had a studio next to his, and the welcome they were given by the Australian painter John Russell, a friend of Rodin and of Monet, all helped to resolve Matisse's uncertainties with regard to painting.

The climate of Brittany was wet, the sea often grey, the countryside sometimes covered with heavy mist. Yet during the summer of 1896, and even more during that of 1897, Matisse's paintings began to glow here and there with fresh, glittering colours. Rocks looked more solid, the sea became foamy and white on the edges (*Rochers de Belle-Ile*, private collection, Paris), the skies were damp and fresh; and in the still-lifes and interiors, he opened windows through which the light poured in to warm the objects placed in a particular spatial order (*Still-life with black knife*), as they had not been seen since Manet.

The Breton serving girl, 1896 (private collection, Paris), and even more *The dinner table*, 1897 (Niarchos collection, Paris), sum up the lesson he had learnt from the Impressionists. These seem to show what the Impressionists had meant, much more than they indicate possible future developments in Matisse. In a timeless greyness, each object and each element is taken and considered in relation to a fluid, but not vanishing, space around it.

Russell, who had given Matisse two drawings by Van Gogh, introduced him to Rodin and Pissarro, whose friendship became important to him, particularly that of Pissarro, whom Matisse often visited – sometimes accompanied by Marquet – and who gave him generous advice that gradually made him recognise and accept his own destiny as a painter to whom colour was of primary importance. Any discussions they had may have concentrated on Matisse's painting *The dinner table*, which had been far from approved at the Salon of 1897, although Moreau had defended it from the attacks of the critics. Pissarro had to help Matisse to realise that colour tones, already identifiable in this painting, could be taken from its pearly atmosphere and its careful composition, which showed the effects of the past decades and of Caillebotte's dubious influence. This meant a remarkable change of direction in Matisse's development, slowly achieved through a series of consistent choices. And in his painting *Kitchen pots and plate of fruit* 1897–98 (The Hermitage, Leningrad), table and objects are not arranged in an orderly way in space but set, rather timidly, in zones of colour, the intensity of which varies.

London and the Mediterranean

At this point, Matisse realised that he must move resolutely away from all that was most familiar, and seek his own way out of what had become a kind of Impressionist scholasticism.

After his marriage he left Paris and went to London, to study Turner's painting, and then, drawn by the climate of the south and its glittering, violent colours, he spent six months in Corsica and six months near Toulouse.

It was at Ajaccio that he saw the Mediterranean light for the first time, and this 'great wonder', as he called it in speaking to Escholier, was to remain with him throughout his life, a source of exultation and excitement.

He now questioned everything he had done so far. In the sunny climate he began to see objects stripped of any atmosphere, isolated from the light and surroundings in which they stood. He seemed to be seizing them, finding and understanding them for the first time, seeking to pick out each colour as it varied in the light, pursuing everything separately with his brush in an effort to define space through colour.

He was starting to explore colour more or less from scratch, because nothing had really been done about it before; he worked alone, tenaciously and ardently, yet also quite lucidly and patiently. This was so in both his outdoor scenes and his interiors (*The sick woman* 1899, Museum of Modern Art, Baltimore), often roughly and unevenly – as regards both rhythm and form – sometimes horizontally sometimes vertically, his brush built up elements that seemed to defy the finished composition, that even seemed hostile to one another, unconnected in the carefully constructed whole; yet every painting now showed a determined, convinced intensity – far more than had been there before.

Fig. 1

Return to Paris

Matisse did not slip quietly back to Paris, taking up the threads of what he had left behind, as if nothing had happened in the meantime. Moreau had died while he was away – an additional reason for breaking once and for all with the Ecole. All Moreau's pupils were now scattered, none of them in academic circles, each going his own way as Moreau had wished. Matisse's own paintings were not at all the kind that would admit him to the Salon, and in any case, he no longer wanted admission to it. His work shows quite definitely that he now had other points of reference: Gauguin and Cézanne, Van Gogh and Seurat.

However, he found an old friend in Paris – Marquet – who had a studio not far from his in the quai St Michel. During the day, the two men used to meet at Arcueil or in the Luxembourg Gardens, to do quick sketches of the vivid life they found there. In the evenings they went to the *cafés chantants* or music halls, drawing the remarkable world they found there with a swiftness and sensitivity that in a way recalls the manner of Lautrec and Bonnard. Manet

1 *The sick woman*
1899, oil on canvas
30 × 15 in (46 × 38 cm)
Cone collection, Museum of Art,
Baltimore

and Degas had for a long time been interested in this world, and Marquet in particular was successful in depicting it. His use of line seems to suggest the Japanese work which had reached Paris fifty years earlier in Madame Soye's *Porte chinoise*, and this was an influence that in the field of graphic art was to be an important one on the Fauves.

Marquet gave Matisse a sense of the instantaneous quality of the line, and Matisse shared with Marquet his own enthusiasm for light as something to reveal colour, and tried to show him the vibrant qualities of the Mediterranean light. Matisse's present way of painting brought difficulties into his life, for he had cut off all his contacts with the academic world of painting in order to follow his own bent. However, it was at this very time that he bought several works by artists who, though differing among themselves, had caught his attention: two pastels by Redon, a work in plaster by Rodin, a painting by Gauguin and, most important of all, Cézanne's *The three bathers* 1879–82, which in 1936 he gave to the Musée du Petit-Palais in Paris. Matisse was a shy man, and never tried to meet Cézanne, but his relationship with Cézanne's work was particularly intense in those years, in spite of Cézanne's ill-concealed suspicion of artists Matisse admired and respected, such as Gauguin or Van Gogh.

What Matisse particularly saw in Cézanne appears in the way he built up his forms through intense colour, freely used, and even more in the internal structure of his paintings, which have an intense rhythm of their own achieved through an orderly sequence of horizontal, perpendicular and oblique brush-strokes. This was one of the lessons Matisse learned from the man he called 'the god of painting', and which may have been impressed upon him

2 *Male nude*
1900, oil on canvas
39½ × 28½ in (100 × 72 cm)
Pierre Matisse collection,
New York

as early as 1895, when the big exhibition of Cézanne's work was held at Vollard's.

At the same time, Matisse felt he must deepen his study of the figure, which was to be a central theme in all his work. He attended the Académie Biette in the rue de Rennes, where Carrière occasionally corrected the pupils' work. The nudes he painted (*Study of a nude*, private collection, Paris), were boldly constructed, set firmly on their feet, the limbs then set closely round a broad, simplified central line, built up from within from pieces of colour–cobalts, emeralds, vermilions–which seem filtered through glass with intense, intimate splendour (*Blue academy*, Tate Gallery, London).

In the rue de Rennes at that time, Signac's *From Eugene Delacroix to Neo-Impressionism* was being read, and Matisse became familiar with its ideas. A few years later this book was to be important and stimulating in the foundation of his own artistic theories.

First attempts at sculpture

Also at that time, Matisse went to a course in modelling in the rue Etienne-Marcel, and while his own nudes seemed to be built up in a sculptural way, he began to study contemporary sculptors, first imitating and then translating a famous piece by Barye, which had also interested Delacroix, *Jaguar devouring a hare*.

Matisse's sculpture was not the opposite of his painting, but its complement. He came to it, not so much through Barye as through Rodin. And in the meantime the way in which he composed his paintings became more careful and more severe, indeed the colours became muted. Perhaps this reflected the practical difficulties of his life at the time. Growing financial pressures made it necessary for him and Marquet to take on the humiliating job of painting yards and yards of a decorative frieze of laurel branches in one of the reception rooms at the Grand Palais.

Matisse's first answer to Rodin's sculptural influence appeared in *The serf* (1900–03), which already showed a concept of modelling that was the antithesis of Rodin's. It was neither strictly naturalistic nor an exercise in anatomical analysis; its obvious expressiveness, its anti-monumental air, link it to the nudes Matisse painted in the rue de Rennes. Something he said about his work at the time is illuminating: 'My working discipline was already different from Rodin's . . . At that time I was already well aware of the general architectural structure, which took over from the details, producing a living and interesting synthesis.' This implied no compliment to Rodin. On the contrary Matisse looked at him critically and found a vital, though controlled, intensity in the tenseness of the material itself, an intensity linked with the rhythms of the surfaces and the enfolding movement of the limbs, as can be seen in the first *Madeleine* (1901).

During these years, while he was first experimenting with sculpture and tirelessly examining the structure of his drawing, Matisse exhibited for the first time at the Salon des Indépendants (1901), then in the first Salon d'Automne (1903) and finally, in 1904, had his own one-man show at Vollard's.

Matisse was having little success, either critical or commercial, when Signac invited him to spend the summer at St Tropez, then a small, undisturbed port. At the time he was painting–apart from his nude studies–everyday scenes and subjects which he sought to give the greatest intensity of colour, as, for instance, in *Notre Dame at sunset* 1902 (Albright-Knox Art Gallery, Buffalo) or in *Bois de Boulogne* 1902 (Pushkin Museum, Moscow), or else he tried to find links between colour and light, as in *The studio under the roof* 1902 (Fitzwilliam Museum, Cambridge) or the tightly modelled *Carmelina* 1903 (Museum of Fine Arts, Boston). After Manet's death, when Impressionism was in a state of crisis, what Seurat, Signac and others were doing and planning seemed actually to worsen the crisis. Impressionism itself had found a subtle way out in the wholly personal work of Toulouse-Lautrec, and Monet, with obsessive obstinacy, managed to catch the eternal mobility of things. This was not an answer to the questions raised by Impressionism, but a sort of dialogue, the meaning of which was to become clear only years later.

Cézanne had nothing to do with this particular crisis. At the end of the last century and the beginning of this, he seemed a solitary figure, quite removed from the rest and with nothing to contribute to questions of painting at the time. His critical re-establishment later was due to Cubism on the one hand, and to Matisse, in a number of ways, on the other.

Impressionism was challenged by the slackened tension of Gauguin's *à-plats*, by the mystical sensuality and proud stylisation of the Nabis, although each of them had developed in his own way; or else by the tragic ragings of Van Gogh, with his clear-sighted madness and longing for self-expression.

Academic painting stood smugly on the one hand; while on the other hand, what has been called 'all the devilry of painting' seemed to confirm the crisis with each individual work produced. In this state of cultural confusion, Manet or Renoir, quite apart from Cézanne, of course, could appear to be revolutionaries, and Impressionism was rediscovered not so much because its discoveries and its language seemed new, but because of the freedom and autonomy of those who opposed it. This opposition was still an anti-conformist reaction, carried as far as possible within the limitations of

**The visit
to St Tropez**

the time, by artists of the future. Among the many things implied in it, one stood out: the lesson of painting itself.

Active, worried, critical opposition did, however, manage to point out the insufficiency and the limitations of Impressionism within the restricted field of naturalism in which it had expressed itself. At this point it was perfectly natural and explicable that Seurat's Neo-Impressionism, with all its theory and all its technical resources, should be the focus of interest for many painters; particularly because of the way in which he composed his paintings, through a knowledge of colour and a great vitality of feeling – both of them highly attractive qualities. Nor was Pointillism unknown to painters like Lautrec, Gauguin, Van Gogh or the Nabis, or, later on, to Kandinsky and Picasso.

Pointillism, then, seemed something brilliant and deliberate to Matisse and other painters whose best work was done during their Fauve period. And for Matisse, who had had a chance of getting to know and to consider not only Neo-Impressionism, but Signac's theoretical work on the subject, and had seen the most eminent artists of the day pass through a similar phase in painting, the summer of 1904 in St Tropez was one of the most important periods of his life. Some lines written by Signac seem almost prophetic: 'The artist whose genius will impose this technique may not yet have appeared among the Neo-Impressionists, but at least they have simplified his task. All this triumphant user of colour need do is appear: the way ahead lies open for him.'

At the beginning of the summer, Matisse felt drawn to examine the structure of Cézanne's painting, and meant to discover the whole range of its possibilities, by studying its volumes and masses. But the sunny climate of St Tropez, which reminded him of his stay in Corsica and near Toulouse, the chance of meditating on the natural world, out of doors, the discussions on colour, the fact of being with friends – Signac, with his solemn, dogmatic theories, and Cross, who was so much easier and more human, and was always ready to understand and discuss Matisse's varying opinions: all this meant that the severity Matisse had used in his compositions during the past few years gave place to a study of colour, out of doors, facing out to sea (see for instance, *St Tropez* (Bagnols-sur-Cèze Museum) and *Paul Signac's* Fig. 3 *terrace at St Tropez* (Gardner Museum, Boston).

On his return to Paris Matisse exhibited fourteen paintings at the Salon d'Automne. In these the progress of his feelings is clear; with short brush-strokes he accentuates the contrasts and corresponding qualities of his colour, which is no longer powdery; the outlines of mountains, sea-shores and roads all stand out solidly against the burning glow of light and colour, the intensity of which makes it seem almost abstract, and no longer describable. In all this, Matisse was clearly opposed to the methods of the Impressionists.

During the next few months his work showed that he was faithful to the principles of Pointillism, which seemed to be confirmed and almost verified in December, 1904, by Signac's exhibition at Druet's.

The bewitching qualities of the countryside around St Tropez had given Matisse a kind of unconscious 'longing for Islands'. This was not like Gauguin's search for freedom far from home, however, Aragon called Matisse 'the man who dreams uninterruptedly', in whose hands 'the poorest, most ordinary things become objects of luxury, indeed, luxury itself'. By this time he had done a preliminary study for *Luxe, calme et volupté* (John Hay Whitney collection, New York) in which, within a broad, rising horizon, the richness and refulgence of nature is shown in burning tones. And at the Salon des Indépendants of 1905, Matisse exhibited the painting that, while it confirmed his fidelity to Neo-Impressionism, at the same time challenged the concept of a geometrical pattern by replacing it with one of colour.

Fig. 4 *Luxe, calme et volupté* (Ginette Signac collection, Paris), named after Baudelaire's lines in *Invitation au voyage* ('*Là, tout n'est qu'ordre et beauté, Luxe, calme et volupté*') was enthusiastically received at the Salon and by Signac as well. Indeed, Signac bought it and kept it in his villa at St Tropez for forty

3 *Paul Signac's terrace at St Tropez*
1904, oil on canvas
28½ × 23 in (72 × 58 cm)
Isabella Stuart Gardner Museum,
Boston

years. This painting did not show a mere passing loyalty, but new reasons for painting itself. Dufy said it showed the miracle of imagination introduced into drawing and into colour; Leymarie called it: 'a conscious use of line and colour, taken as far as they will go; a transitory stage but one essential to the birth of Fauvism'.

For a year Matisse was an ardent *pointilliste*, as his friend Puy confirmed; and at several levels of conviction and intensity, the other artists in his circle followed him: Marquet, Camoin and Manguin, who also chose St Tropez for their working summer in 1905, and those who seemed to work more independently of the group – Vlaminck, Van Dongen and Valtat.

The Salon des Indépendants itself, by putting on a large retrospective exhibition of Seurat's work that same year (1905) seemed to have picked on the point where all the experiences of contemporary painters were converging, and to have acted as a kind of catalyst to them. Even Braque was involved in it, and produced his own subtle and delicate brand of Pointillism.

Collioure

Under the guidance of Signac's principles, the group at St Tropez had produced its ideas on colour. The following year Matisse went to Collioure, a small port near the Spanish frontier, where he was often to return during the next ten years, and it was here that the ideas of the Fauves were to germinate and mature.

As president of the executive committee of the Salon des Indépendants in 1905, Matisse had asked for Derain and Vlaminck to be shown at the same time as friends who were closer and more congenial to him. These two painters were at the opposite end of the movement, both in the independent

4 *Luxe, calme et volupté*
1904–05, oil on canvas
37½ × 45½ in (95 × 116 cm)
private collection,
Paris

way in which they had developed and sought to paint, and in Vlaminck's exhibitionistic tendencies. But Matisse decided to take Derain with him to Collioure for the summer.

Matisse was eleven years older than Derain and may have felt invigorated by his youthful enthusiasm. At the same time Derain could appreciate Matisse's meditative qualities, his patient, lucid methods of study, his humanity, his courage, and the encouragement he gave others. Indeed, it is clear that Derain acted as an active mediator between Matisse and Vlaminck, seeking to overcome the difference between the two not wholly divergent painters.

Derain's letters from Collioure to Vlaminck at Chatou are a valuable guide to this period which came immediately before the upsurge of Fauvism. Both Derain and Matisse were filled with enthusiasm for the landscape, which inspired them to keep painting in a way that made colour the most important thing about their work; yet they also concentrated on painting the figure, making portraits of each other. Matisse said: 'What concerns me most . . . is the figure,' because it allowed him to express his almost religious feeling for life.

In Derain's letters we can follow the phases of the development of himself and Matisse while they were at Collioure, and the important moments through which they came to find a solution for their problems. Among the points they dealt with was the concept of light and shade as 'a world of clarity and luminosity that is opposed to sunlight'. This was something that had so far been neglected by them both, but in the future it was to become what Derain called 'a return of expression'; and later he observed that with

Matisse beside him it was possible to be rid of 'all that was superficial in the division of colour,' which may harm the things whose 'expression comes from deliberate lack of harmony'.

When Derain finally came to say, with regard to Pointillist painting, that it was a 'world which, pushed to the absolute, destroyed itself,' he had quite clearly gone beyond the influence of Signac and Cross, which he had felt through Matisse. Matisse, on the other hand, was suffering from a crisis that settled itself much more slowly, since he was always inclined to pay fully for any experience he had had, and anything it brought him in its wake.

What is quite certain, in any case, is that one of the elements that helped his Pointillist phase to come to maturity was the Mediterranean world, which rekindled the memory of what he had learnt in Corsica and near Toulouse some years earlier. In several landscapes, such as *The port of Abaill-Collioure* (private collection, Paris), the short brush-strokes, with their rhythmic variations of length and intensity, still remain, as they were to do to some extent for the next few years; but it was the tone that gave life to contrasts of colour, and built up the images into a harmonious whole.

Fig. 5

This exuberant colour reached its height in landscapes like *Trees at Collioure* (Lehmann collection, New York), and paintings of figures, the most important of which is *Woman in a hat* 1905 (Mrs Walter A. Haas collection, San Francisco). This scandalised people at the Salon d'Automne of 1905, for its colours had little to do with a naturalistic view of the figure: green tints both broke up and built up the face, holding the balance between the broken colours of the dress and the bold, outsize framework of the hat.

The boldest influences of style seemed to come to Matisse through Van Gogh and Cross, but he did not yet manage to achieve an inner harmony through the use of colour to build up the image. At this time of tension, Matisse became aware of a new influence that in some ways was to be crucial. Once more, he became aware of Gauguin's work and then decided to 'repatriate Gauguin' in the new vision of his painting.

At that time, the only paintings of Gauguin which Matisse had seen were a few works shown to him by Vollard, and those in the short retrospective exhibition hurriedly assembled for the first Salon d'Automne just after his death. But during their stay at Collioure Matisse and Derain had seen a good deal of Maillol, who, although he had started in the decorative tradition of the Pont-Aven group and the Nabis, was, by the time Matisse met him, working on designs for tapestries and starting to work as a sculptor. This meeting was important for Matisse, not just because Maillol was full of pagan joyousness and enchanting talk, but—much more—because it was through him that Matisse came to know the work of Gauguin. Maillol not only talked a great deal about Gauguin—his exotic experiences and his achievements as a painter—but introduced Matisse to Daniel de Monfreid, who had been Gauguin's most faithful supporter and had a fair number of splendid paintings of his, most of them still unknown.

In these, what must have been a revelation for Matisse was not merely the fact that Gauguin rejected all the experience of the Impressionists and Neo-Impressionists who, in rejecting what has been called 'the mysterious centre of thought', had ended up with scientific explanations, but the contrast

5 *The port of Abaill-Collioure*
1905, oil on canvas
$23\frac{1}{2} \times 58\frac{1}{4}$ in (60 × 148 cm)
private collection,
France

between him and Cézanne, his efforts to achieve a synthesis, and above all the *à-plats*.

Meeting Maillol, and discovering all the exuberance of his talk and his pagan view of nature, must have given Matisse the idea for the large painting he was to work on during the winter, the famous *Bonheur de vivre*; and getting to know Gauguin's work precipitated the crisis in his own work in a definitive way.

A number of Matisse's paintings from that summer at Collioure seem to be strung between two extreme alternatives: the *à-plats* on the one hand and the technique of the Neo-Impressionists on the other. But it is also true that whatever technique he uses – oil, watercolour or drawing – the images acquire an obvious, new luminosity and prove he was achieving a synthesis through abbreviating the forms he used.

He must also have known Cézanne's work during the past few years, because in the portraits he painted when he returned to Paris, although the images have an intense colour that makes them non-naturalistic and stresses their expressive qualities without losing their careful, proud construction, every part of the painting tended to acquire an unexpected quality. The hierarchical sub-divisions of attraction vanished, and each part achieved, instead, a rhythm of its own – one that was close-knit but autonomous.

Fig. 6   For this reason too (consider the *Portrait of André Derain*, Tate Gallery, London), each individual part of the portrait is accentuated in a way that makes it unusually expressive. Matisse knew the dazzling, mysterious and ancient art of mosaic already. Indeed, during his Pointillist period it became, in a sense, a part of his own work. But, in the exciting crowd of influences and comparisons, he must have found other images, other tastes with a flavour of the East, to which his ideas of colour could be linked to give each human image its own enigmatic, vibrant individuality. It was on the human image that he now concentrated, with a renewed sense of commitment, and as he contemplated his model he remembered Gauguin's invitation to reconsider a new, exciting reality. All this settled Matisse's destiny as a painter for ever.

In order to achieve what he called 'the condensation of feeling that makes the painting,' he was not content to make a single effort at a painting. With his logical, disciplined nature, he said: 'I prefer to add to it in order that I may be able to recognise it later as a representation of my spirit.' Finally, the choice of colour no longer depended on any scientific theory; it was founded on 'the observation, the feeling and the experience' of his own sensibility. Composition, to him, meant the art of combining the elements he had available in a decorative way; this work converged into a single, complete harmony, in which 'every superfluous detail takes on, in the spirit of the man looking at it, the place of another essential detail'. This was the time in which he had to go back to the essential principals of human communication: 'It was the point of departure of Fauvism: the courage to rediscover the purity of methods.'

The Salons of 1905

The Salon des Indépendants, which originated in 1884, had another intensely interesting and lively period just after Manet's death, when Matisse and his friends began to exhibit there in 1904: Marquet, and then Manguin and Puy; Friesz, Dufy and Camoin; Van Dongen and Valtat; Derain and Vlaminck and, finally, Braque. But although such progressive artists took part in it, this annual show was limited by one of its rules, which said that participation was open to all. Obviously this meant that the works submitted varied a great deal in quality and that mediocre painters were encouraged, although not explicitly, to submit their works.

The idea of the Salon d'Automne of 1903 was born out of the need for another kind of show, one that was selective. This was started by the architect Jourdain, and run by a jury elected in rotation, supported by Rouault, Marquet, Vuillard and by the most eminent artists of an earlier generation: Cézanne, Renoir, Carrière, Redon.

6 *Portrait of André Derain*
1905, oil on canvas
15 × 11 in (38 × 28 cm)
Tate Gallery,
London

The new Salon was more open to new ideas and to the latest experiments in art, and was held at a different time of the year from the Salon des Indépendants; and as it was held in the autumn, painters who had been working out of doors during the summer were able to show their latest works there. The first year it was held in the basement of the Petit Palais, but from 1904 onwards it was held in the Grand Palais, and it was then suggested that not only painting and sculpture should be shown, but a selection of all the arts—architecture, music, the decorative arts. Both Salons put on exhibitions of work by artists which were still unknown or little known to the public; these aroused a great deal of interest and response from painters. Particularly important were those of Lautrec, Seurat and Van Gogh at the Indépendants, and of Gauguin and Manet at the Salon d'Automne. Matisse exhibited at the Salon d'Automne from the start.

It seems significant that an exhibition of Ingres's work, sixty-eight of his works, and one of Manet's work, about thirty paintings, were held at the Salon d'Automne of 1905. Other exhibitions like these, at both the Spring Salon and the Salon d'Automne, had shown that taste and culture were moving stormily ahead. In 1905, when the Fauves appeared as a group for the first time, with all their new ideas and possibilities, there seemed to be no points of reference, no connection with the past; everything seemed quite different and quite divorced from it.

It is not very difficult, today, and it may be useful as well, to find links between Matisse and Manet; but even in the case of Ingres, it is not hard to see some connection with Matisse's work. Delacroix once told David that in a painting the head ought not to be more noticeable than the fabrics or the accessories, that all its parts should be equal; and Matisse applied this to Ingres, being strongly drawn to paintings which Ingres himself had called minor, but which, from Seurat to the Cubists, were much more attentively regarded: the nudes, the portraits and the drawings. Matisse himself said that 'drawing is the probity of art', as it must possess 'a force of expansion that makes the things which surround it alive'.

That year, the ageing painters who had supported the founding of the Salon d'Automne exhibited their most recent paintings: Cézanne, Redon and Carrière. The Douanier Rousseau was there too, and so very noticeably, were the ambiguous Nabis who, as a group held together by Symbolism, had by then ceased to exist. But what was most remarkable about that Salon d'Automne was the extraordinary outburst of bold, new, violent colour. Not only Matisse, but Marquet, Manguin, Puy, Valtat, Vlaminck, Derain, Van Dongen, Friesz, and Rouault all exhibited. In the foreign part of the Salon the Russian section, put on by Diaghilev, was extremely important. In it, two artists then working in France, Kandinsky and Jawlensky, whose use of colour made it seem likely that they would soon come close to the Fauves, exhibited. But it was the Fauve group that drew upon themselves the most attention and anger, indignation and scandal. The heroic days of the official Salon, when it had outraged academic opinion, seemed alive again.

'A paint pot has been flung in the face of the public,' said C. Mauclair. Nothing as new and revolutionary had been seen since the rise of Impressionism.

It does not really matter where the name Fauve originally came from. It appeared, was used to describe a particular, short-lived period, and was immediately recognised as identifying it. Vauxcelles, the critic of *Gil Blas*, is said to have been standing in front of a small neo-fifteenth-century statue by the sculptor Marquet, threatened on all sides by aggressive-looking paintings, and to have remarked: 'Donatello among the wild beasts!'; but Rouault maintained and Lassaigne confirmed it, that Matisse himself in an extremely hairy overcoat gave rise to the comment: 'Just look at the fauves!'

All the names and stories connected with this scandalous and exciting start seemed quickly to turn into myths, and it was Matisse who paid most dearly, as far as the critics and the general public were concerned, for appearing as he really was: that is, as the most convinced member of the group which was initiating everything that was to follow, although his mad, 'eccentric' use of colour made even the critics bold enough to support him in the first place feel desperate.

The open window (Mr and Mrs John H. Whitney collection, New York), the *Woman in a hat*, a still-life, two portraits of his wife, a landscape, two watercolours and two drawings all gave offence through their bold, vehement use of colour and the way they rejected any naturalistic use of it. The famous portrait of his wife called *Portrait with a green stripe*, 1905 (Rump collection, Copenhagen), which in form is noticeably dry, in its coloured parts is balanced by à-*plats*, from the red of the dress to the blue-black of the hair, against a background of contrasts and relationships; and the simplified face is divided into two by bold green brush-strokes separating the part in light from the part in shadow.

Fig. 7

Matisse's friends and colleagues had done no less than he had, on the whole. All the Fauves reached artistic truth by avoiding the limitations of reality, and by justifying their paintings through form and colour, not through any direct connection with nature.

On balance, the Salon d'Automne of 1905 proved to be successful for the Fauves, and the scandal, the disappointment and the indignation it aroused

7 *Portrait with a green stripe*
1905, oil on canvas
$15\frac{3}{4} \times 12\frac{1}{2}$ in (40 × 32 cm)
Statens Museum fur Kunst,
Copenhagen

were in proportion to its success. Among the critics who wrote about it was André Gide, who, though he admitted Matisse's 'fine natural gifts', saw his paintings as 'figures in a theorem', in which everything could be deduced and explained, even the fact that they 'went to extremes'. Gide added that art, which meant moderation, could not be found in these extremes.

In the few years between 1905 and 1910, Fauvism finished what it was trying to do. But it also pointed out a new way in which art could progress and expressed the individual tensions of its members, quite apart from what the transient group was doing as a whole.

The group was to have an unexpectedly large influence on contemporary art, for all the artistic currents of our time have been based on a similarly subjective view of painting, and a similar freedom of invention and operation. In the Fauves this seemed startling and almost offensive to a shortsighted critic (V. Pica) at the Salon d'Automne of 1907, who said they had an 'ill-tempered delight in ugliness, which [made them] despise the study of forms, the relationship of planes, the gradations of colour and the gracefulness of drawing' and that they liked 'to copy the faults of Cézanne and Gauguin and the intemperance of Van Gogh'.

Obviously it is much easier for us today to see what this movement meant, where its origins lay, what its choices were. Its origins were mixed and paradoxical, including Irish miniatures, Japanese prints, and medieval stained glass; a mixture of colours, filtered through Daumier and Delacroix; and some freely chosen influences: a little of the young Manet, Cézanne, in some ways, Gauguin, for some of them, Van Gogh for others. Indeed, the group can almost be divided into two, depending on which of the two latter

8 *Study for 'Bonheur de vivre'*
1906, oil on canvas
16 × 21½ in (41 × 55 cm)
Haas collection, San Francisco

painters influenced them. Gauguin influenced Matisse, Marquet, Dufy, Friesz, and Braque; Van Gogh influenced Vlaminck, Derain, and Van Dongen. But this division is really much too definite. The two groups merged, their outlines overlapped, and neither Gauguin nor Van Gogh really influenced their development – rather, they had made available a climate in which painting could exist independently of outside pressures, as what Maurice Denis called 'pure painting, the pure act of painting'. Nor must we forget that Neo-Impressionism was an important influence upon the Fauves, indeed that it acted as a catalyst.

In spite of Vlaminck's claim, it was Matisse who was the real animator of the Fauve group during its tumultuous existence, and it was he who, throughout the 'immense parabola' of his working life, remained faithful, in his spirit, to the Fauve instinct. He and his friends, unlike the Impressionists, looked 'at things, not beneath things', and the sunfilled paintings they produced gave a new, so far undiscovered dimension to the joy of life.

Whatever imagery he may have used, whatever his technical expertise, the cultural experiences he underwent or the way in which he developed his style, this theme – the joy of life – was always the fundamental motif of Matisse's work: the exultant sense of an inner harmony, the conscious optimism of wisdom. In his early Mediterranean pictures he had already sought it, in *Luxe, calme et volupté* he had partly expressed it; but in the summer of 1905, and in the winter months that followed, he tried to express this feeling – the fullness of life which he had experienced – in his painting.

In *Pastorale* 1905 (Petit Palais, Paris) he had already caught, in the Arcadian enchantment of particular places, man's eternal, happy intimacy with nature, through the use of sunshine in his colours and forms; but the same feeling appears more deeply and more intensely in the many studies for his *Bonheur de vivre*. Seurat and Signac had already suggested the same kind of thing, but Matisse's freer and bolder use of colour went beyond anything they had done.

All the myths and all the magic he had found during the summer in the sea and in the woods of Collioure were transferred to canvas, in definitive, monumental paintings, during the winter. In March 1906 he had a one-man show at Druet's, but its success was soon overshadowed by the admiration his *Bonheur de vivre* (Barnes Foundation, Merion, Pennsylvania) aroused at the Salon des Indépendants. This painting quite definitely showed Matisse's convictions with regard to art, as well as his aesthetic ideas and his spiritual and intellectual condition. The colours were related to one another in a disciplined but always surprising way, in violent, immediately striking flat areas of colour which were never static and meant 'expression', not 'im-

Fig. 8

9 *Still-life with red carpet*
1906, oil on canvas
$35\frac{1}{2} \times 45\frac{1}{2}$ in (90 × 116 cm)
Musée de Peinture et de Sculpture,
Grenoble

pression'. Superficially, no lines seemed to be used, but in fact a linear rhythm held the painting together, as if the colours clung naturally together and thus produced the forms. In this painting the joy of living is glorified as the highest form of wisdom and, after Matisse's heart-felt search for pure painting, his imagination bursts through it. Once again, as in *Luxe, calme et volupté*, of 1904-05, a painting that in every way anticipates it, the Arcadian motif cannot, of course, be found in the sense it had in the ancient world. Instead, it is transformed into a kind of fairyland, the first and the greatest in our century, and one which includes the whole poetic idea of Fauvism and the whole of Matisse's work. Intimate, inexhaustible, going beyond the optical excitement of colour, it has a vibrancy that seems to express Bergson's '*élan vital*'. What Argan has called the expressionism of joy appears in the actual tension of each colour, which yet manages to maintain the balance of a rare poetic harmony.

The allusion to the theme of Cézanne's *Bathers* is quite clear, as it was in a number of earlier sketches and studies, and in *Pastorale*; but the difference in the way Matisse worked, his inventiveness and the way he proceeded pictorially, is also obvious. He did not seek to make the images progress in contrast to one another, with the space around them balancing them and making a necessary, integrated whole; instead, he created a nucleus of sunfilled colour, irradiating outwards and able, on its own, to justify the figures flung into space, the lines spreading outwards, the colour contracting inwards.

In the summer of 1906 Matisse made a short journey to Biskra in Algeria, before his usual stay at Collioure. He was inspired to make it, as Renoir had been, by Delacroix's painting *Algerian Women*.

The discovery of Islamic art, the visual and tactile enjoyment of Arabic objects, fabrics and ceramics, nourished and invigorated Matisse's loving

The journey to Biskra

delight in the exotic more directly than the Japanese prints had done.

In that year, his still-lifes (*Still-life with geraniums*, Art Institute, Chicago) show richly coloured objects, their forms simplified but their surfaces sensually tactile; and his figures (*The reader*, Musée des Beaux-Arts, Grenoble, a portrait of his daughter Marguerite), reveal an inner sense of construction, through which the coloured areas and the compact outlines are balanced. In the first version, and still more in the second version of *Young sailor* (Seligman collection, Basle), this imposes a curvilinear rhythm that recalls Oriental patterns.

Having caught the light, Matisse's colour plays on tone and contrast, and is boldly used. Sometimes a colour is barely hinted at, sometimes it deepens or becomes fluid, or is suddenly splashed with intenser tones, flung down as in *Still-life with red carpet* (Musée des Beaux-Arts, Grenoble), or marvellously balanced, as in *Still-life with melon* (Barnes Foundation, Merion).

Fig. 9

The secret of this hidden harmony, which dominates even the most furiously Fauve-like paintings, lay in Matisse's suspicion of what was merely instinctive, in his belief that every really active feeling had a logic of its own, and could be patiently filtered through reason.

The Salon d'Automne of 1906 was a firework display in which all the Fauves took part—not just the faithful old colleagues but a number of newcomers. And, at the same time as this dazzling show, the Gauguin exhibition was held. Matisse himself refused to confirm it, but the fact remains that, while the Nabis absorbed Gauguin's influence as if by magic, the Fauves really appreciated what he had taught them and took it over in a critical way. Their glowing flat areas of colour, arbitrarily chosen yet linked in a surprising, formal way, meant that each image was its own symbolic representation of itself; in the foreground of the composition it was supremely important, but it was used in such a way that the very space around it became part of the rhythm of the images.

The sense of action was thus dealt with, and the composition achieved a unity through the synthesis of form and colour, and new dynamic possibilities which, Matisse himself said, must be seen 'as a whole' because 'everything in a painting that has no function is harmful, to say the least'. This is not the place to discuss the events of the first ten years of this century, when the most important movements and artists in contemporary art first appeared; but what is quite certain is that, although Fauvism inclined towards action, artistically speaking, more than towards aesthetic programmes, and so was more provocative, more forward-looking, than theoretical, ideologically it concentrated on promoting exchanges and using past experiences in a new way.

Fauvism appeared outside Paris. There was the Brabançon Fauvism of Rik Wouters, and Kandinsky's subtle, delicate and intricate version of it, with its origins in the special nature of his experiences and influences in France. Kandinsky's precious, enamelled use of light and colour came at the same time as it did in Matisse and his friends, even when he was entirely on his own, as he was at Sèvres in 1906, pursuing his own personal and solitary brand of Fauvism. There were not merely these kinds of Fauvism, but a Fauve group which exhibited for the first time in Dresden in 1906. The date is worth noting. Among the group were Kirchner, Heckel, Schmidt-Rottluff, then Amiet, Pechstein and, more independently, Nolde; and there was also Van Dongen, who acted as a link between this Dresden group and Paris.

At the start, it was almost a coincidence that Fauve painters were appearing in other places, a coincidence brought about because certain painters found they had certain needs and demands in common, and came together in ways that socially and culturally appeared provocative. Later the groups came to know one another, and to exchange methods and ideas, although these were limited by differences in their artistic as well as cultural and ethnic backgrounds. Today, it is hard to say just which group came first, or which ideas preceded which. Both the French and the German groups had similar influences behind them, similar ancestors; the German painters, like the French, had been influenced by Van Gogh and Gauguin, and by Pointillism. But their direct links were forged only in 1907, when the Germans met the French Fauves directly, after Pechstein had visited Paris and had come to know them.

Some of Matisse's work in this period is of particular interest and importance for what it shows of the visual and cultural influences upon him, resulting, as it does, from his personal experiences and explorations. *Blue nude* 1907 (Museum of Art, Baltimore) is one. This painting is the key to the Pl. 6 understanding of his work at the time. Its decoration has something Arabic about it, which recalls his first feelings on visiting Algeria. The palm tree holds its own among the buildings, and the flowers seem to be trying to suggest a space that is wholly invented, wholly conceptual. Against the bluish lights, which become heavy shadows, and reflections that emphasise the expressive tension of the nude, is the figure, the movement of the hips counter-pointing the strangely shaped shoulders, between a line that hinges upon it and is finally resolved in the more subtle, more delicate outlines of the resting hand, the ankles, the face marked with blue and black. There is a clearly expressionistic tone in it, but this is not marked by joy or by any dramatic feeling; rather it comes from the emotional content drawn from the plastic and formal elements of the painting, indeed from the compositional contradiction between the exotic decorations and the powerfulness of the image.

It is, indeed, by presenting so many different elements in a contradictory way – elements that are not even strictly necessary to one another, stylistically speaking – that Matisse once again showed that he refused to accept a natural relationship with real facts, and that he meant to restore and strengthen his images according to his own ideas of invention.

'Expression,' he wrote in his 'Notes d'un peintre', 'is not found, as far as I am concerned, in the sudden appearance of passion on a face, and does not assert itself with a violent movement. It is in the whole composition of my painting: the place the bodies occupy, the empty spaces that surround them, the proportions: everything has its own function.'

Once again, a date helps to point out some interesting events in Matisse's progress. 1907 was the year in which Picasso finished *Les Demoiselles d'Avignon*, and it was not merely chance, or merely to commemorate the death of Cézanne, that the retrospective exhibition of his work was held at the Salon d'Automne that same year. Indeed, this exhibition in a sense helped to disperse a group, while it seemed to indicate, and to establish, the formation of Cubism.

That Salon d'Automne was in fact the critical period for the Fauves as a united group, and Cézanne's presence there made clear how frail and how short-lived were the movement's ideas. It showed the limitations implied in their belief in the expressive power of pure colour, in some cases used to the point of satiety. It showed their faith in the instinct, carried to lengths that threatened to make them repeat themselves; and it showed the thinness, or even the non-existence, of any ideological ideas, concentrating, as they were, upon the need to break with Impressionism as well as with sterile official attitudes. It showed the Fauves' lack of interest in the scientific problems of the time, and in the scientific advances going on around them. All these limitations were to be found within Fauvism itself, even in its more positive aspects, and at the same time, just because they are inextricably part of it, they are also the reason why the movement broke up.

In considering this break up, Cubism may appear to be a kind of brutal reaction to the Fauves' avoidance of ideological commitment. Indeed, it did seek to establish itself upon theoretical foundations that had been checked and carefully considered, foundations that did not avoid the implications of what scientific research and discovery had produced in the first ten years of the century. But Fauvism shared in the responsibility for promoting the new current of ideas, in particular because it had expressed the spirit of freedom and had hoped for a new order and a new direction in art. Matisse had already felt the influence of Cézanne. So had other painters who were drawn to Cubism but were determined not to let themselves be caught up in it, and who went back to study Cézanne when the excitement over the Fauves was over, but their effect still lingering. Finally, we must not forget the influence, admittedly controversial, of the small statues and wooden masks from the Ivory Coast and the Congo which had been circulating in Paris since 1902, and were 'discovered', first of all, by the most alert members of the Fauve group, who had taken from them not only the strength achieved by using images in a new form, but a disciplined, careful freedom of composition. Derain and Vlaminck had, in fact, already seen and admired the Negro sculptures in the British Museum, and indeed had bought some African masks for themselves. Matisse bought one in 1906, with an enthusiasm he must have communicated to Picasso when they met, as they often did, at the Steins'.

The Fauve group dispersed, and each member of it had to make his own way and prove himself. The colours which Derain had called 'dynamite' in the hands of the Fauves were used phonily by their imitators, the minor Fauves who were to dominate the Salons d'Automne for the first quarter of the century.

Fig. 10 On the other hand, it was at the Salon of 1907 that Matisse exhibited his first version of *Le Luxe* (Musée d'Art Moderne, Paris), painted at Collioure during the summer, while the second version (Statens Museum fur Kunst, Copenhagen) was painted during the winter of 1907–08. In these paintings Matisse's style was recomposed into a single harmony of relationships, sensitive decoration and colours used in particular areas determined by lines that had no naturalistic meaning. Once again, Matisse used Baudelaire's theme, and between the first and second versions of the painting he reasserted in his freedom of composition, his long-considered, long-acquired faith in the value of his own methods, the kind of optimism Argon called 'the luxury of great men'. The first version sets each element in its own radius of action, through the conclusive, circular harmony that links the curvilinear outlines of the horizon and of the sea with the rhythm of the figures. The second shows that Matisse had returned decisively to flat colour areas, capable of drawing all images to a single centre, and rejecting any attempt to define them in any kind of hierarchical way in space.

The most fertile and important period in Matisse's working life now began, in the very contradiction between his own ideas and those of the group that had called him its leader. Unlike some of the others, whose greatest creative inspiration had come from the Fauves, Matisse showed that Fauvism, to him, had been a crucible of experience and inner discussion. Indeed, it might be said, paradoxically and exaggeratedly, that Matisse identified himself with Fauvism to the extent that he was not a Fauve: he was not an attacker but a watchful, logical frontiersman, able to rationalise each instinctive impulse, so that, particularly in his paintings but in his writings as well, he was able to express the movement's fleeting, fragmentary and easily lost aesthetic thought.

Notes d'un peintre In December, 1908, Matisse published his 'Notes d'un peintre' in *La Grande Revue*. These were personal confessions rather than theoretical ideas, but they can be identified with the aesthetic of Fauvism and remained valid throughout Matisse's life, as the poetic ideas that supported his painting.

He wrote of the search for means of expression, between the twin poles of colour and drawing; of a classical education and the need to take over, 'entirely personally', the work of the Old Masters; and finally of the knowledge and influence of Eastern art. He wrote of simplified drawing, which generated light, the result of a great deal of labour at the end of which 'no correction [was] possible'. Bouguereau, at the Académie Julian, had shown little foresight when he scolded Matisse for carelessness, and called him a man who would 'never know how to draw'.

10 *Le Luxe*
1907, oil on canvas
$82\frac{1}{2} \times 54\frac{1}{4}$ in (210×138 cm)
Musée National d'Art Moderne,
Paris

This lucid, firm way of working was explained in a significant passage: 'Remarkable effects can be achieved with colour by the use of similarities and contrasts. Often, when I begin to work, I feel things freshly and superficially. Until a few years ago these feelings were often enough for me. If, today, when I am sure that I see reality more deeply, I were to be satisfied with them, I would have something indefinite in my painting; I should have put down fleeting sensations, linked to a particular moment that would not encompass me completely, and which I would find it hard to recognise the following day. I want to reach the condition in which feeling is condensed: this is the essence of a painting. I might be content with something done quickly but I would soon tire of it; I prefer to re-elaborate it, so that later on I may recognise it as representing my own spirit.'

Later he wrote: 'The signs I use must have an inner balance that means they do not cancel one another out. In order to obtain this balance I must put my ideas in order; the relationship between the tones must exalt rather than annul them.' He said he worked 'without theories', but was aware of being urged on by an idea that developed as the painting progressed – logically. 'I think one can judge an artist's vitality and strength from the degree in which, directly impressed by some natural sight, he is capable of organising his sensations and finding his spirit in the same condition on other occasions . . . This power means that a man must be master of himself, must be able to impose some discipline upon himself. The simplest means are those which allow the painter to express himself in the best way.' This seemed to confirm what Moreau had forecast about him: 'You will simplify painting'. So, painting a picture could be as logical as building a house; the human side should not concern a painter; it was either there, or it was not; but 'if one has it, it colours the work in spite of everything'.

This personal manifesto found its expression in Matisse's paintings at the time; particularly *Sculpture and Persian vase* (National Gallery, Oslo), *Bathers with tortoise* 1908 (Joseph Pullitzer Jnr. collection, St Louis) and *Draughts players* (The Hermitage, Leningrad), in which lines are simplified and abbreviated in what Lassaigne called an intense effort to achieve 'exalted purity'. Indications of what is happening in nature or in space are given by cutting lines dividing earth, sea and sky on the horizon, elements distinguished by their essential colours, green and blue; and between them the brown tortoise or the shiny black spherical draughts are set, very carefully. In his 'Notes' Matisse wrote about perspective, saying that objects were placed on various planes in their luminous space – 'therefore in perspective, but in a perspective of feeling, a suggested perspective' – suggested, above all, by the need to give each element of the whole construction its own role, equal with the rest. This was a fundamental premise in Matisse's later work and in his ambitious plans for murals that were soon to be stormily fulfilled in *The dance* and *Music*, painted for Shchukin.

The same subjects treated again

At the Salon d'Automne of 1908, Matisse exhibited a decorative panel he had painted for the Russian collector's dining room, and some paintings, sculptures and drawings that showed how he had been progressing recently. Together these conclude a period of research, but the stimulating inventiveness of his best works in this period is more important than their particular dates.

An old theme Matisse had loved when he was first reconsidering the Impressionists is found in *The dessert, harmony in red* (The Hermitage, Leningrad), dated 1908. The curves, suggesting a kind of Art Nouveau elegance, become much more than mere ornament; indeed, they draw the whole of the large vermilion area towards the foreground of the canvas. The highly visual space spreads and contracts in the splendid arrangement of objects with their simplified lines and, even more, in the mixture of colours. The woman herself is, like the rest of the elements in the painting, a synthetic part of the visual whole that is so full, so striking, that it confirms Matisse's concept of a 'living space'. On the left, the chair seems to have lost all its own perspective, swallowed up by the greedy colour; the landscape outside the window is also drawn to the red harmony of the interior, the related colours, those of the house and sky, and of the small feathery trees which seem to be borrowed from Persian miniatures.

The speed with which Matisse worked, the multiplicity of his responsibilities and interests, seemed to increase and concentrate his qualities; and the synthesis he achieved in each painting seemed unique and unrepeatable each time. A portrait of his son, Pierre Matisse (private collection, New York), uses a technique of abbreviation to achieve its effects, and this is found again, even more importantly, in the sumptuous *Still-life with coffee pot, carafe and fruit bowl* (The Hermitage, Leningrad), in which there are blue curves over the whole surface of the canvas, which produce a thrusting movement in the undulating cloth, a movement stilled by the unexpected punctuation of the objects on it.

The exotic atmosphere of these paintings was not the result of what Aragon called 'a longing for Islands'; nor was it the kind of thing Apollinaire described in 1909: 'one is surrounded by works of art ancient and modern,' he wrote, 'by exquisite fabrics and by sculptures in which the Negroes of Guinea, Senegal and Gabon have shown the wildest passions with rare purity'. Rather it consists in an unusual use of reality, which Matisse transfigures in an imaginative but not excessive way, and this moderation exists in him in spite of the apparent passions and excesses in his paintings, because each element suggests the 'values necessary to the composition'. Matisse worked calmly on his paintings and continued to work around them 'until this calm [was] part of the painting itself'.

When the model or the costume worn by the model suggested some ethnic or folkish circumstance, Matisse did not emphasise it. This can be seen in *The guitarist* 1903 (Ralph Colin collection, New York) and in *The gypsy* 1906 (Musée de L'Annonciade, St Tropez), the most shockingly Fauve of his paintings, according to Lassaigne, in *Mme Matisse in a Manila shawl* 1911 Pl. 14 (Offentliche Kunstsammlung, Basle), and in the superb series of odalisques over the next few years. Matisse wanted to avoid stressing this particular element as pictorially important; instead, he wished to use each motif as part of his style, which obeyed its own exclusive harmony, and had no room for escapist themes and preconceived ideas. 'A work must carry its whole meaning in itself and hand it to the spectator even before he knows the subject of the painting.' Matisse's serious vision produced exotic allusions beyond any representative analogies, even though these might be quite obvious, and thus it asked those who looked at his paintings to keep a firm hold on what he intended to do in them. 'I dream of an art that is balanced, pure and tranquil, without worrying or disquieting subjects, an art that will give the intellectual worker, the business man or the literary man a sense of relief, that will calm his mind, rather in the way a comfortable armchair relaxes him when he is physically tired.' He wanted to restore to each man his share in the harmony of the world, a harmony that could be promoted by the well-ordered arrangement of forms in their related colours, as in *Still-life with geranium* 1910 (Staatsgalerie, Munich), in which the rhythmical arrangement of the objects and the glowing colour connected with that rhythm together produce their visual effect.

Panels for Shchukin

As Reynal remarked, 'the mystery of Matisse's amazing magic lies somewhere between his imagination and his gold-rimmed spectacles,' and this is what makes his unexpected use of colour plausible and acceptable. Without this capacity to recreate, the decorative panels for Shchukin's room, *The dance* and *Music* would have been unimaginable. Both were shown at the Fig. 11 Salon d'Automne of 1910, as the idea they contain had long interested Matisse, and he had planned to decorate an ideal atelier on three floors. In these plans he had even decided on the role of the colours: 'The blue of the sky, the pink of the bodies, the green of the hill,' to achieve 'a compositional serenity obtained through the simplification of ideas'.

The curving cadence of *The dance* seems to come from the radiant centre of *Bonheur de vivre*. Argan considers this work to be Matisse's serene though negative answer to Cubism, to Picasso's 'calculated' foray. Cubism analyses the object rationally, whereas Matisse synthesises everything intuitively, and each part of the panels is upheld by a strong creative intelligence that intensifies the theme by using essentially simple methods and the purest possible colours. Perhaps more than any other of his works, these panels challenge the pictorial principles of Impressionism; the light has no natural origin, its incandescent artifice comes from within the form, in fact from the fusion of form and colour.

When Berenson, who had met Matisse at the Steins', visited his studio, he was particularly interested in these dancing nudes, which seemed to him 'the nearest thing to a great work of art that Matisse [had] ever produced'. This limited praise was provoked, as it happens, by Berenson's knowledge of Pollaiuolo's *Dancing nudes*, which he had discovered in the Torre del Gallo in Florence. But the comparison between the two paintings was merely casual; superficially their motif was similar, but the methods used to express

11 *The dance*
1910, oil on canvas
$102\frac{1}{4} \times 154$ in (260×391 cm)
The Hermitage, Leningrad

it were completely unalike. In Pollaiuolo, the energetic movement of the bodies seems to be trying to communicate the dynamic effect of their un-resolved tension to the space around them; whereas in Matisse's panel, the simple, curving lines suit the movement of the nudes, giving them an endless, circular rhythm broken only by the curving cadences of the arms, alternating with the tapping of the feet grafted into the curve of the hill. The horizon is low but the blue sky is entirely submerged in the sunlit order of the dance, and the two-dimensional space makes this Pan-like event wholly understandable, an event in which the antithesis between Apollo and Dionysus seems caught and resolved.

The static equilibrium of *Music* corresponds to the dynamic equilibrium of *The dance*. The figures are arranged stilly and carefully, as in an archaic song. Nothing disturbs what might be called their monodic tone and the flat but solid outline of the bodies fits into the continuous, concise and abbre-viated line. The figures also seem to appreciate the dense colours, in other words, they appear to appreciate what Gowing has called the 'essential irrationality' of Matisse's use of form in this painting.

The atelier and journeys

These years were not only intense and happy because of the fertility and full-ness of Matisse's creative life. Other events and new relationships enriched it.

For some time the Steins, Marcel Sembat and Hans Purrmann had sup-ported his work, financially as well as in other ways. Sarah Stein, who had supported him since 1905, and Purrmann, in 1908 asked him to open his atelier at 33 Boulevard des Invalides, once a convent of the Sacred Heart order, to pupils.

In 1907 Matisse went to Italy for the first time, as he wished to see the work of Giotto and Piero della Francesca. He must already have seen and been influenced by the exhibition of French primitives at the Marsan Pavilion in Paris in 1904, and perhaps since then had been influenced by the painting of Jean Fouquet.

In 1908 he spent the summer in Bavaria, and in the same year had his first exhibitions abroad. In New York, Moscow, and Berlin, and at Cassirer's, where he had a flattering success. Indeed, when he went to Munich in 1910 with Marquet to see the exhibition of Islamic art, he realised how famous he had become. Those years were important, artistically, and it is worth recalling a few events that took place at the time: the founding of the Neue Kunstler-vereinigung, promoted in Munich by Kandinsky in 1909 and, in 1911, the birth of the Blaue Reiter, and Die Brücke's move from Dresden to Berlin.

In 1911 Matisse made a short trip to Moscow to see Shchukin's splendid collection, but he was interested above all in the icons. A few months earlier he had been on a trip to Andalusia, and in 1912 and 1913 made two long visits to Tangiers. These biographical events are not meaningful in themselves, but show Matisse's desire to see Oriental culture, from Islamic to Byzantine art, as one of the origins of Western art. From 1909–17, although he kept his home in Paris, he spent most of the year in the country at Issy-les-Molineaux, on the road to Calmart. He wanted to meditate, to clarify his style still further, he needed to get away from Paris and the possibility of being conditioned by his surroundings.

In those years, Matisse's activity as a sculptor was interesting and lucid. The need to model had nothing to do with the ease with which the material is modelled; it came from the urge to make the material itself cling together in order to free the form, to involve it in space with a dialectical purpose that came from the slow, structural use of planes.

New efforts at sculpture

It is significant that sculpture appears often in Matisse's paintings, almost as if it forms a part of them (see, for instance, *Goldfish* 1909, Statens Museum fur Kunst, Copenhagen; *Sculpture and Persian vase* 1908, National Gallery, Oslo; *Pink statue on a red sofa* 1910, Pushkin Museum, Moscow; *The studio* 1911. Pushkin Museum, Moscow). *Reclining nude* 1907, on the other hand, must be considered with that fundamental painting *Blue nude*.

In 1909, he made *The snake-dance*, confidently carried out, with the curve attracting the empty space, and between 1910 and 1913 he made five versions of *Jeannette*. But it was the work he did on *Nude from the back*, begun in 1909, taken up again in 1913 and then in 1916, and finally between 1926 and 1929, which seemed closest to his painting.

Matisse's sculpture does not, in fact, show the kind of narrow pleasure in beauty that Berenson seemed to charge Matisse with when he reproached him for being influenced by Cambodian sculpture, several pieces of which he found in his studio. Matisse, however, did not seem to take this criticism to heart. In order to achieve a sense of the exotic, he had no need to escape to a lost paradise; his bold, lucid, well-ordered imagination could give a rare, exotic and primitive air to anything that came its way, even before he had actually discovered these qualities in reality. What was exotic in his work was not to be found in metaphor, or in elements transposed from other works, even if they had been studied and had proved stimulating. It lay, rather, in the authoritativeness of his choice, the risks involved in his feelings, and finally, in the Cartesian yet exalting clarity of his style.

Often, in both painting and sculpture, the subjects are repeated. There are, for instance, the famous variations of *Goldfish* (1909, Statens Museum fur Kunst, Copenhagen; 1911, Pushkin Museum, Moscow; 1911, Museum of Modern Art, New York), in each of which, around the tactile, liquid water that gives the fish its vitality, each other object and element, recognised with a kind of slow, surprised pleasure, states that it has a secondary role. Or there is his *Still-life with aubergines* 1911–12 (Musée des Beaux-Arts, Grenoble), a glorious feast of *à-plats* and daring yet successful comparisons, in which even the window does not confine the inexhaustible decoration indoors, but leads to new, flaming colours outside. And there are the mysterious blues of *Blue windows* 1911 (Museum of Modern Art, New York), in which he seems to be foreseeing a night in the distance, a night that, as if by magic, alters the familiar objects standing against the various cobalts and the stylised, post-Art Nouveau trees. Matisse did not yet know the nights of Tangiers, but here they seem to have been used in advance, as if he had merely to rerecognise them in the future.

Pl. 12-13

This same force is expressed through his imaginative choice and pictorial rigour in *The painter's family* 1911 (The Hermitage, Leningrad), which is composed with the hierarchic, innocent wisdom of a Byzantine mosaic or perhaps of a page from a Persian miniature. The decorative part—in which slithering planes are slowly, gradually overturned, their varied arrangement balanced by the two women at opposite ends of the painting—is poured out with increasing intensity: from the flowers flaking out on the ivory of the walls to fade away in the centre, on the white decoration of the stove, counterpointed by the contrasting materials of the sofas at the side, and falling at last on to the rich carpet that reabsorbs the frail wooden elements of the chairs and table. Further points of reference are the two small boys' red suits and the girl's big black dress, broken slightly by a few touches that revalue black by using it as a colour; and finally the small heads which seem to be cut out, like the ivory ones in Japanese fans.

In this way, familiar interiors are reinvented with an extraordinary, intimate vitality, because, in fact, as Reynal rightly remarks, Matisse substitutes the reality of the imagination for the reality of appearances. For this reason it is an exciting adventure to 'enter' his studios. The *Red atelier* in the Museum of Modern Art in New York (1911), with its harmony of colours suggested by the title, is filled with objects Matisse loved and, like other paintings of his, with his own works. In *The studio in Moscow* 1911 (Pushkin Museum) the space, in the vanishing perspective of the pinkish-ochre floor, is not so much defined by the yellow and blue diagonal on the carpet as articulated by the vibrant way in which the objects are treated: vases, modelling tables, the flowered screen, the famous bunched blue cloth, and, scattered about the room, works by Matisse himself–pieces of sculpture, paintings, sketches and, receding on the right, one end of *The Dance*. The window, which is visible behind the screen, is another square within a square, curtained by foliage that suggests a background of Pointillism in a free sort of way. Matisse often used things like the square within a square in his paintings; he often picked up something he had already used in the past and took it further, well aware that there was no stopping the possibilities that might arise, the situations that might develop. *Nasturtiums* and the panel *The Dance* 1912 (Pushkin Museum, Moscow) show this clearly. Apart from the touches of crimson and green, yellow and blue in the objects, the way he paints the dance on the sloping walls shows how he had arrived at methods lighter, more precise and more delicate than those in the panel in Leningrad.

'To me,' Matisse had written in his 'Notes', 'expression does not lie in the passion that appears suddenly on a face or shows itself in some violent movement. It is in the whole arrangement of my painting: the place which the bodies occupy in it, the spaces around them, the proportions, everything has its part to play.' These convictions formed the fundamental basis of the way he taught the pupils who came to his atelier in Paris. They also clarify the exclusively pictorial meaning of the word 'expression' (not its existential meaning, which was used in the Brücke group) and confirm the quality of his style, a quality that was above all subject to an intellectual order which synthesised ideas quite outside, or contradictory to, the naturalistic order.

In Morocco   For this reason, Matisse's visit to Morocco was not an escape–admittedly, Morocco was more accessible than it had been to Delacroix or Renoir, but it was still exotic. However, this was not what Matisse found there; it was rather as if he made the journey to rediscover feelings that were already vibrantly sustained by his imagination and his intellect. It is significant that *Blue window*, as we have already said, seems to have been suggested by ideas of distant places; yet it was painted before he went to Morocco with Marquet and Camoin.

On his return, Matisse exhibited paintings and sculpture at the Bernheim-Jeune Gallery, in April, 1913. There had been long intervals between his shows in France. There was the one-man show at Druet's in 1906, and the retrospective exhibition at Bernheim-Jeune's in 1910, but abroad his fame was spreading. For instance, he had an exhibition of sculpture in New York in 1912, at Gallery 291, and took part in the Sezession in Berlin and the Armory Show in New York, Chicago and Boston in 1913.

The Moroccan paintings shown at Bernheim's were quickly scattered among collectors, who were more often foreign rather than French.

This intellectual strictness, which simplified things progressively more and more and reduced them boldly to essentials, while keeping their poetic

12 *The gate of the Casbah*
1912, oil on canvas
$45\frac{3}{4} \times 31\frac{1}{2}$ (116×80 cm)
Pushkin, Museum,
Moscow

meaning and substance, and which had appeared in *Blue window*, was already found in a painting that preceded Matisse's visit to Morocco. This was *Zorah standing* 1911 (Pushkin Museum, Moscow), in which the flat, icon-like appearance of the image is so elongated that, from the top of the head to the yellow Turkish slippers, it scarcely fits into the canvas; and this use of a two-dimensional image seems to give it a sort of ritualistic feeling somewhere between the Byzantine and the barbaric. This same barbaric touch appears with almost Fauve monumentality in the two versions of the Moroccan man, standing and seated. In *Moroccan standing* 1913 (The Hermitage, Leningrad and at the Barnes Foundation), the outlined parts in colour are exalted by the reduction in its form.

Matisse's Moroccan paintings can be grouped together, for their style has remarkable unity, and an intense, careful sobriety that no attractive fluency disturbs. Matisse controls the brightness of these places with the lucidity of his own mind, through the personal way in which he relives the past.

A Tangiers landscape seen through a window, *On the terrace* and *The gate of the Casbah* (all three 1912, Pushkin Museum, Moscow) are fundamental in showing this. The first picture, in which the swollen blue landscape seems to invade the bluish inside frame of the window, is broken by the clear light

Fig. 12

masses of the houses and the ochre vase on the window sill. The second, with its delicate pink and bluish light, turns on the small female figure whose light weight in the curving rhythms seems enough to hold down the receding blue carpet. The third, in which the Moorish shape of the arch is reabsorbed in the frankly anti-naturalistic colours, fading amazingly from blue to pink to green, has a ghostly vanishing figure that seems to fade into them.

In these paintings Matisse's colours are more profoundly and intensely sober than before; yet they often glow with a rare, luminous quality. They lack what Raynal called the 'simultaneous, then fiery, reactions' peculiar to many of his earlier works and to many after 1917.

The lessons of Cubism

Matisse now showed an increasing interest in the lessons learnt from Cubism. This can be seen in his more meditative attitude, and in his inner determination to exercise a more severe control over the composition of his paintings. Not only those already mentioned, but others painted after 1913 show this. For instance, his *Portrait of Mme Matisse* (The Hermitage, Leningrad) or the *Portrait of Yvonne Landsberg* 1914 (Philadelphia Museum of Art) or later the *Portrait of Greta Prozor* 1916 (private collection, New York), all reveal it in their greater use of monochrome, which shows more clearly the importance of line in the construction of the painting. However, in the lines of Yvonne Landsberg's portrait, and in the energetic quality implied in the pose, Gowing finds traces of a Futurist influence. On the other hand, as far as this portrait is concerned, Matisse's own words seem explicit: 'The lines in the portrait of Miss Landsberg are structural, and I put them around the figure in order to spread the space further.'

In any case, Matisse's interest in Cubist painting had been confirmed already, in paintings before 1916, which showed how everything more obvious and accidental in the other works of that year had been superseded. For instance, *Still-life with oranges*, 1912, shows in the swelling coloured areas, the use of lines rising from the horizon and the bold use of the vertical, not only that Matisse was interested in methods found in some Japanese painting, but that he was also, in a way, re-reading Cézanne through Cubist eyes.

Insofar as it was a movement of art and ideas, Cubism did not influence Matisse a great deal. But the discoveries of Cubism over the past ten years did allow him to analyse objects intellectually, without seeing colour as the primary consideration. This was a matter of intellectual research, an effort to achieve the balance of a synthesis between space and composition. A reported exchange between Matisse and Michel Georges Michel may not be strictly true: 'Do you understand the Cubists? I assure you *I* don't,' Matisse is reported to have said. 'Of course not, Matisse,' Michel replied, 'since you preceded them'. But what is certainly true is that just before *Les Demoiselles d'Avignon* appeared, Matisse had in his *Bonheur de vivre* proclaimed the unchanging intelligence of beauty; and, from the time in which the Fauves as a group were scattered until the end of his life, he never ceased to celebrate the joy of his own cosmic intuition. Cubism, a tangential movement as far as he was concerned, touched him only insofar as it coincided with his interest in composition at the time; indeed, it confirmed the autonomy of his vision, for, although it strengthened his belief in the need for order in space–even geometrically achieved–it did not make him renounce the bolder, subtler qualities of colour.

Berenson's hasty, brutal judgement of Matisse ('after racing shoulder to shoulder with Picasso in the art of the last fifty years, he has finally come in second') is not only critically sterile in setting the two painters up against each other, and tends to confuse human situations with artistic values, and rivalries, either real or imagined, with the most varied facets of twentieth-century culture, but ignores what Picasso himself has said. Admittedly, there is something histrionic and visionary about Picasso's view of himself, but he admits Matisse's independence of style and ideas: 'Everything, really, comes out of ourselves. There is a sun in our belly with a thousand rays. Nothing else

13 *The Moroccans*
1916, oil on canvas
71¼ × 109¾ in (181 × 279 cm)
Museum of Modern Art,
New York

matters. This is why Matisse is Matisse. He has a sun in his belly.'

Matisse's most famous painting from 1916 is certainly *The Moroccans* **Fig. 13**
(Museum of Modern Art, New York), which synthesises the visual and
emotional sensations of his visits to Africa with what he had discovered about
compositional rigour. As he looked back with detachment, his memory re-
ordered each element through geometrical forms that gave particular
emphasis to representative and spatial values, shown above all in green and
mauve zones, between a large, glowing black texture. The balance of colour
is directly related to the harmony of the elements, which seem to take on an
emblematic value in Matisse's own vision, which, according to Brandi, is one
of integral colour made into space.

Colour, especially green and black, continued to dominate Matisse's
paintings and to synthesise his ideas of composition. This was so in *The
painter and the model* 1916 (Musée d'Art Moderne, Paris) or in *Woman in an
armchair, Lorette in a green dress* (Galman collection, Lomas, Mexico), which
came from the same period. The painting's harmony is achieved not only by
the intense restraint with which colour is used, but by the solemn severity of
the elements, by the insistent rhythm of the vertical lines. This is also the case
in *Studio on the Quai St Michel* 1916 (Phillips collection, Washington), where
Matisse returned to paint during the winter from 1914 onwards. It can also
be seen in the clear way in which space is arranged in *Piano lesson* 1916
(Museum of Modern Art, New York), in which the surface of the canvas is
lengthened as much as possible by the vertical greys between which sober,
sonorous colours are spread, counterpointed horizontally by the curved
balcony railings and the carved woodwork, behind which, surprised and
bewildered in a highly abstract synthesis, appears the archaic mask of the boy.

The music lesson 1917 (Barnes Foundation), another version of the same
subject, is more colloquial and familiar, more feeling and blooming, less
severe. *The gourds* 1916 (Museum of Modern Art, New York), achieves an
exalted severity, however, and both *The lemon* 1916 (Barnes Foundation)
and *The tin jug* 1916–17 (Cone collection, Museum of Art, Baltimore) have
roundly defined forms. In the latter painting the background, with its
glowing, dusty-pink curtain, is picked up in the objects which are marvellously tactile, while the black retains one of its rare chromatic qualities,
its capacity to accentuate and exalt the intensity of every other colour.

Black quite often seems to dominate the space, a precious setting for Matisse's **The first**
glowing colours. This is so in *Interior with blue violin* 1917–18 (Statens **stay at Nice**
Museum fur Kunst, Copenhagen), one of his own favourites. The light does
not enter the room through the shutters to illuminate the colours, but their
deep glow gives the indoor light intensity, since to Matisse, lack of direct

light did not mean lack of lighting but a purifying filter for every colour. Through the window we catch a glimpse of the sunny diagonal of the raised shutter, and of the sea at Nice, which Matisse had rediscovered at a time when he was in poor health. Once again he had caught the Mediterranean sun, although only from a modest studio he was using in the Hôtel Beau-Rivage. The following year he returned there, and at last, in 1921, although he kept a studio in Paris, he moved to a house in the old part of Nice.

Happiness nourished his spirit again. This was not due merely to success, but came in particular from a sort of loving gratitude for the natural glory which he had rediscovered. 'When I realised I would see that light every morning, I could not believe in my own happiness,' he wrote.

It was not the easy delight in finding subjects for his painting, although from time to time he did work out of doors with bright colours, on the hills around the town (for instance *Landscape at Montalban* 1918 (private collection, New York); nor any anxiety to consider particular problems of style, although he enjoyed his friendship with Bonnard at Antibes and his cordial, spontaneously happy meetings with Renoir.

There was more than this. Against the background of this intermediate period in his life, somewhere between 1917 and 1926, there was the living vitality of a man who had put his whole self into painting, who was strung up as far as he could be; and at that time any solution of his problems would have seemed disappointing, or at least risky.

What is certain is that he did not betray the exercise of painting itself, but gave himself up to a simpler, gayer, more imaginative and less difficult freedom in it. The post-war years were, psychologically, a period of post-ponement, when time had to be spent on the burning problems of the day. The abstract tension that had appeared in Matisse's work during the past few years slackened, and he relaxed and expressed himself naturally, sometimes with a certain virtuosity. Leymarie wrote of this: 'His creative genius is not as pliable as people often try to make out it is.'

White feathers was painted in 1919. Apart from the version at Minneapolis Institute of Art, a number of drawings and another two versions of it exist: at Goteborg Museum, and in Washington, at the National Gallery. In the beauty of Antoinette, the model who was then his favourite, in the lightness of the feathers and the black velvet bows which Matisse himself had arranged, even in the detached, conventional pose, he exalted the function of the line.

Matisse's paintings now showed a natural grace, a simple direct sensuality that came from his gay, familiar surroundings, full of decoration he loved, objects he knew well. This is so in *The painter and the model* 1919 (Harry Bakwin collection, New York), in which the woman is already posing with the soft languorousness of the odalisque in *After the bath* 1920 (Albert D. Lasker collection, New York); or else an easy intimacy, shown in particular in *Tea in the garden* 1919 (David L. Loew collection, Beverley Hills), with its varying shades of green.

Occasionally though Matisse painted something more thoughtful and serene, even though he expressed it with direct, persuasive familiarity, as in *Persian women* 1919 (Barnes Foundation) or even more in *Large interior at Nice* 1921 (Art Institute of Chicago), where the simple, foreshortened space is crossed by vertical and diagonal lines, while the figure on the balcony suggests a greater visual distance when compared with the sea's horizon. Effects like these become even more remarkable in the strange contrasts of colour, set off once again by black, in *The open window, Etretat* 1921 (Bernheim-Jeune collection, Paris).

Yet even in those years, when he seemed to have stopped searching, Matisse did not stop trying to distil his exquisite colours, and the combinations of colour, rich to the point of virtuosity, producing masterly paintings like *The Moorish screen* 1922 (Philadelphia Museum of Art) with its rich, inventive decoration, a soft delicate background to the conversation of the two women. Perhaps even better examples of his use of colour in this period are his series of odalisques: for example *The Hindu pose* 1923 (Donald S. Stralin collection, New York); *Seated Moorish woman* 1922 (Barnes Foundation); *Odalisque with raised arms* 1923 (Art Institute of Chicago).

In the warm sunny climate of Nice, Matisse tried to keep contact between the interior and the exterior, in spite of the shutters, which were often half closed. It was not a case of concentrating on the problem of illumination, or of giving a greater sense of depth, it was that he tried to give this contact a symbolic meaning, to make it a link between reality and imagination. The poet André Rouveyre, who was a friend of Matisse's, explained this: 'The shutters appear in his canvas as an object that stands between his unbounded country and his private country, an object that forms a boundary, yet can be moved . . . It is here that his field of spiritual and visual sensuousness begins, his thoughtful feelings, his bravura performances with colour; and here that images of women, either dressed or nude, appear, always subordinate, however, to something latent or imperious in him: the sovereignty of the principles of his own art.'

More sculpture

Matisse recovered his creative energy around 1925, when he turned once again to sculpture and once more found both his fertile inventiveness and his natural pictorial exuberance, in the great period from 1925–32.

The *Large seated nude* (1923–25), in which the figure is leaning boldly backwards, in an unexpectedly natural movement, emphasised by the firmness of the planes, is matched by a painting from 1926, *Odalisque with drum* (William S. Paley collection, New York), in which a densely arranged composition is illumined by the red, and by other jewel-like colours.

The way in which Matisse recovered a density of form in his paintings can be seen in those where the decoration is controlled by the composition, which in its turn is modified even more by the monumental character of the main image. This is so in his *Decorative figure against an ornamental background* 1927 (Musée d'Art Moderne, Paris) which appears stiff and solemn, bronzed and remote as an idol, in the pattern of triangles made up of the pose itself and cunningly used in relation to the space available, in a great profusion of flowery walls, carpets and objects which, while steeping the painting in colour, bring everything back to the harmony of the dominating tones.

Perhaps Matisse controlled his luxuriant decoration more successfully in *Odalisques playing at draughts* 1929 (Ralph F. Colin collection, New York), another version in the Stockholm National Museum); in *Woman wearing a veil* 1927 (William S. Paley collection, New York); in *Lemons on a tin plate* 1927 (N. Cummings collection, Chicago); in *Nude with blue cushion* 1927 (Sidney Brody collection, Los Angeles); and in *Reclining nude from the back* 1927 (private collection, Paris) in which, as Leymarie expressed it, he 'kept a balance between the severe concentration of the forms and the wildness of the decoration'.

Large grey nude 1929 (Beyler collection, Basle) seems to show a quieter ornamentation in order to maintain the formal quality in the figure. That this balance is always dangerously hard to achieve, and yet in fact can be successfully found, is proved by *Girl in a yellow dress* (Museum of Art, Baltimore), begun in 1929 and finished in 1931, in which the bewildering wave of colours, from vermilion floor tiles to variegated draperies, is freed by the almond-like form of the woman who seems isolated as she faces all that surrounds her.

In those same years, Matisse worked on his *Large head* 1927, which is quite obviously a very sculptural portrait, and later returned to his *Nude from the back*, whose form, emerging from the background, seems to have the solemn expressiveness of primitive sculpture. This was in line with his efforts to find a new and simpler synthesis in painting. As he put it himself: 'I have sculpted like a painter, not like a sculptor.'

These ten years of work might at first sight appear the most contradictory period of Matisse's life. In one way he was attracted by the fertile, easily used methods at hand; in another he was determined to settle the antithesis between construction and decoration. Early in the decade he was influenced by Renoir, who was living near him at Cagnes, and as a result of this contact his colours became more remarkable than ever. Yet, although he did not give up his rhythmical use of decoration he sought, through his experience of sculpture, to reconcile any discordant elements that might arise.

The dance at Merion

During those ten years, Matisse travelled. He made two winter trips to Normandy, staying at Etretat in 1920 and 1921, and visited London in 1920 and Italy in 1925. In 1927, he won the Carnegie Prize, and was then asked to sit on the jury at Pittsburg in 1930. This was his chance to make a long journey. But before going to the United States he spent three months in Tahiti.

It is hard to say what his discovery of the Polynesian world must have meant to him—the vast, unspoiled, irridescent spaces in which his unconscious 'longing for islands' could at last be satisfied. He did not paint while he was there, he drew, but the glowing beauty of Tahiti enriched his memory and his inventiveness for the rest of his life. He called Tahiti 'the paradise of painters', but staying there did not mean he was escaping, either from himself or from others. He was not there as an expatriate, but in the paradise regained of his own imagination. He drew, he collected objects, seaweed, flowers. Everything helped to increase his remarkable collection of images, to add to the forms and colours that were to appear luxuriantly in his memory and his desire, in the paintings of the next few years.

In the United States he met Albert Barnes, who already owned many of his paintings, and was given the chance to paint something ambitious and monumental: a large rectangular room in the Barnes Foundation at Merion, a surface of 52 square metres, not counting the windows, divided by three arches which supported the ceiling. Matisse was enthusiastic about the project, a difficult one because of the problems of composition and arrangement. He refused to use models and sketches and, in order to work on such a large scale, he rented a disused cinema in Nice.

The theme of *The dance*, already taken from the throbbing centre of *Bonheur de vivre*, and used several times over, gave him a new inventiveness which he himself described: 'For some time I had been thinking of the representation of this dance; I had already put it into *Bonheur de vivre* and then into the first large composition. Yet when I tried to make sketches on three canvases each a square metre, I could not do it. At last, when I took three canvases, five metres in size, the same size as the walls, and used a piece of charcoal stuck into the end of a long bamboo cane, I began to draw fast, feeling a rhythm within me that urged me on. The surface was already drawn in my mind.'

The graphic rhythm was born in a miraculous-seeming way, with spontaneous cadences. But as far as colour and its effects were concerned—grey, black, blue and pink—Matisse for the first time used a method that was to become entirely his own and definitive during his final years of activity: the *gouaches decoupées*, panels of painted paper cut out according to whatever shapes the form demanded.

When the work was finished, he realised that through an error in calculating the size of the panels, it was impossible to put it into place. This painting was later bought by the Musée d'Art Moderne in Paris.

He now had to start his monumental work all over again. He kept the same theme, which was very important to him, but did not repeat the rhythms that he had used before; instead he developed the idea with inexhaustible creativeness.

The images of the first version, although their movements and positions were so free, seemed to fit the full sweep of the arch. But in the second version there were more of them—more figures, more rhythms—bursting out fluidly and gracefully yet controlled by the careful lines around them, in exultant rhythms which the semi-circular arches seemed unable to contain fully. This meant that, quite beyond the limitations imposed by the building itself, the dynamic tensions of these wild rhythms could be imagined.

In 1933, Matisse went to Merion for a second time in order to set up his work. The contrasts of colour and rhythm were integrated, and necessary to one another. As Barnes himself has shown, the colour applied on large areas help, with the line, to revalue the effect of the drawing. It is, in fact, the unity of colour that intensifies the composition of the painting, so that gradually 'the element of pure decoration gives way to the expressive value of the form'.

Between 1933 and 1934 Matisse produced few works, but among these few were important paintings like *The magnolia branch* (Museum of Art, Baltimore) and *Portrait in a white dress* (private collection, Paris) which foreshadowed the dazzling renewal of his painting in 1935.

The dream (private collection, New York) used the line in a subtle, essential way, but the fundamental work of 1935, the painting that really showed Matisse's style in a definitive way, was the superb *Pink nude* (Cone collection, Museum of Art, Baltimore). Many drawings and twenty-two photographs document the way Matisse developed it; first simplifying the forms, finally reaching a coherence and unity in his composition that was close to that of his most recent works, such as *The dance* at Merion. Equally coherently, he said in 1936: 'It was the point of departure of Fauvism, the courage to rediscover the purity of methods.' This richness of invention, backed by a simplification of the forms, is found in the cartoon (Catou Museum) he made for a tapestry commissioned by Marie Cuttoli 1935 (private collection, New York), *A window in Tahiti*, which dazzlingly recalled his memories of Polynesia.

Matisse still celebrated the beauty of the female form, but gave it a new kind of ritualistic appearance. The line was now significantly flowing, colour was flat and even, and a solemn enchantment was achieved in the image through a kind of limitless natural alteration of form. This is so in *Lady in blue against a black background* 1937 (John Winterstein collection, Philadelphia). Other images seem to identify their elegance with the controlled fluidity of the curve, like the figures that were to decorate a drawing room of Nelson Rockefeller's house; or they seem to simulate a musical score as in *Music* 1939 (Albright-Knox Art Gallery, Buffalo).

The exuberance of natural and decorative elements in *Interior with an Etruscan vase* 1940 (Museum of Art, Cleveland) takes over the whole atmosphere of the picture, actually appearing to undermine the stability of the table, through the use of an unexpectedly flexible black plane. In *Anemones and pineapples* 1940 (Albert D. Lasker collection, New York) the decoration is shrill and at the same time delicate, with a tactile quality about it.

The years from 1941 until Matisse's death, after an operation in 1954, were a time he always considered an unexpected piece of good fortune. In spite of physical suffering he managed to express his spirit's gratitude through feverish activity, and with a determination to work that bore witness to his unfailing joy in life. At Cimiez, and then at Vence, in the villa La Rêve (which really was a dream of his imagination) he lived and worked in enclosed places, among precious objects, oriental silks and curtains. Finally, in 1949, he went back to the Hotel Regina in Nice, where he had lived before.

Red still-life with magnolia (Musée d'Art Moderne, Paris) was an exuberant painting with which to open a new period; in a way it contrasted with other still-lifes such as *Still-life with oysters* 1940 (Kunstmuseum, Basle), painted a little earlier, and with a cleaner, tidier composition.

Pl. 34

Paintings of figures reappear, in the *Dancer, Rococo armchair, black background* 1942 (private collection, New York), and complex variations on the theme of figures in interiors, such as *The lute* 1943 (Sidney F. Brody collection, Los Angeles) or *Girl in a fur, ochre background* 1944 (private collection, Paris).

Fig. 14

While he was making cartoons for tapestries, which were then woven at

14 *Dancer, Rococo armchair, black background* 1942, oil on canvas 19½ × 25½ in (50 × 65 cm) private collection, New York

Beauvais, and, in 1946, providing decorative motifs for fabrics for Ascher, all on themes that recalled the enchantment of Polynesia, Matisse went back to gentle, abbreviated curving rhythms, interestingly foreshortened in *Rococo armchair* 1946 (private collection, Paris) and once again explored the secret enchantment of colour indoors.

This series began with *Red and blue interior* 1946 (Musée des Beaux-Arts, Brussels), but there are also small-scale variations on the theme, such as the wonderful *Small blue interior*.

Fig. 15

In *The pineapple* 1948 (Alex Hill Corporation, New York) colours burst vibrantly out and the forms are swollen; *Interior with Egyptian tent* 1948 (Phillips collection, Washington), is a new, coordinated excuse for decoration to be used with dazzling profusion, emphasised by the rhythmical black background, and in an abstract, two-dimensional way which is solved at last by the way in which the table is placed.

Plum tree branch, green background 1948 (Albert D. Lasker collection, New York) also has these qualities of reduction and concentration, and in *Large red interior* 1948 (Musée d'Art Moderne, Paris) they are used almost convulsively. This is a painting that seems to sum up and celebrate the whole of Matisse's pictorial development. The intensely untidy objects give a kind of dynamism to the room, and two of Matisse's own works stand out against the walls, providing a spatial rhythm and contrasting with the light and colours–again, paintings within a painting.

This crescendo–the series of interiors–ended Matisse's paintings in oils, apart from a portrait painted in 1951. But the fact that he gave up painting at an easel did not mean he ceased to exercise his art or his creative powers. On the contrary, he was seeking and creating new methods of communication and of expression.

Comment j'ai fait mes livres

While he was working on the grandiose plan for *The dance* at Merion, he was preparing illustrations with equal enthusiasm for Stephane Mallarmé's *Poésies*. The work was commissioned in 1930, carried out the following year, and published by Skira in 1932. The twenty-nine etchings do not so much illustrate the text as renew and transfigure the very structure of the book. The illustrations appear to have been made fast and easily, but in fact they are the result of careful thought and the patient use of Matisse's graphic gifts. In his *Comment j'ai fait mes livres* he wrote: 'I have described how I proceed; this in no way presumes that there are no other ways, but mine has been formed naturally and progressively.' Later he continues: 'I have forgotten an important piece of advice: while you are working, put your work aside twenty times, and if you need to, start again until you are satisfied.' In this way the mind controls and dominates any possible indulgence of feeling or the senses, seeking to adhere closely to the reality of one's own style, not to natural reality, since, as Matisse himself said, 'exactitude is not truth'.

Matisse's drawing is the purest, the most direct translation of his feelings; but everything is achieved by a constant refinement of methods, until it reaches its final simplification, so that when the drawing has shown light on a white page, he has nothing to add: 'the page is written, no further correction is possible'.

What Matisse wrote in his 'Notes' in 1908 about drawing is relevant to his book illustrations, undertaken in what Marchiori called 'a harmonious graphic relationship within the classic Bodoni tradition'.

Mallarmé's poems were followed in 1941 by Ronsard's *Florilège des amours* and Henri de Montherlant's *Pasiphäe*; The *Lettres d'une religieuse portugaise* were published in 1946 and in the following year Baudelaire's *Les fleurs du mal* and André Rouveyre's *Repli*, as well as several other, less demanding, works.

Of all the works Matisse illustrated the most interesting, for its inventive use of colour and the way it treated its forms, is undoubtedly *Jazz*, published by Tériade in 1947, on which Matisse had begun working enthusiastically in 1944. Against backgrounds of a single colour, clear outlines are boldly cut, extremely synthetic and at the same time open to the light. They themselves are dazzlingly light, in a rhythmical counterpoint in which music and painting seem to mingle.

From 1948 to 1951 Matisse worked on the Dominican Chapel of the Rosary at Vence; this involved a complex labour that included architecture, painting, stained glass, objects and ornaments. In fact, he said: 'The Chapel gave me the chance to realise what I had been seeking by combining them all together.' Matisse was then eighty and took on a work that he considered 'the last stage in an entire lifetime of work, and the apex of an enormous, sincere and difficult effort'. Indeed, he felt that everything he had done until then could only be a preparation for this work.

The chapel at Vence

His main preoccupation 'was to balance the presence of a surface of light and colour with that of a full white wall, covered with black drawings'. Inside a clear, almost slender architectural sheath, colour came from the light filtered through green and yellow stained-glass windows, while on the other three walls images, signs and symbols were set on a white ceramic background. The three groups of figures behind the altar were the tall solemn picture of St Dominic (half of it repeated on the altar-frontal in the church of Assy, also 1948); the Virgin and Child among stylised clouds shaped like large flowers on the long wall; and the via Crucis in the interior of the façade, made up of simplified images and symbols of the Passion.

Fig. 16

This was a careful concentration of Matisse's style, achieved patiently, with special attention to the drawing–the brush stuck into the end of a bamboo cane–and with the will to follow it through to the end, transposing his designs on to enamel and stained glass, seeing to the colours of the glass, the form of the lead. He was tirelessly enthusiastic, with the kind of fervour that made him exclaim: 'Work is heaven.'

In order to obtain that kind of spiritual communication with others, beyond life–'I want those who come into my chapel to feel purified and freed from their burdens'–he conceived a spatial and decorative unity in what was described by Marchiori as 'an immediate and profound relationship, lit up by a mysterious, pagan happiness'.

The black against gleaming white did not describe things, it evoked them. It evoked them in the meaningful tension of its outlines, in the images, which were elongated in an expressive, hierarchical way, in the non-natural, exotic tufts of cloud gathered like flowers around the Virgin, in the hasty-

15 *Pineapple*
1948, oil on canvas
$43\frac{3}{4} \times 33$ in (116×89 cm)
Alex Hill Corporation,
New York

looking, harsh, agitated drawings for the Passion.

Apart from everything else in the chapel at Vence, from the floor to the liturgical objects, and the external belfry, Matisse also modelled his last piece of sculpture for it: the crucifix for the altar, in which there reappears a hint of what Argan called 'the rhythmical theme of the profane and pagan Serpent'.

The gouaches découpées

The flower-clouds of the long wall at Vence, at once exact and imaginative, seem, in their inventiveness, to suggest the technique of the *gouaches decoupées*.

Matisse had used these *gouaches decoupées*, an original technique that was all his own, when he was illustrating *Jazz*, and even earlier, to experiment with the effects of colours in his Merion projects; they were not part of his research but an autonomous tool in his painting. He once confessed: 'When I shut my eyes I see objects much better than I do with my eyes open, because then they are without their minor accidents: it is that which I paint.' These words apply to the *gouaches decoupées* perhaps even more than to many of his oil paintings; indeed, they throw light on their origins and their nature, and on their exciting, simplifying qualities.

He used them from 1944 onwards, but particularly from 1950 to 1954, when his physical suffering made it impossible for him to work in any other way. Yet they were not substitutes for other forms of work, not complementary to other forms, or compensatory. Indeed, the papers which Matisse himself coloured before using them, in order to obtain the exact colour he wanted for his idea, and then cut out with scissors, were the result of a new wave of youthful creativity.

They were *gouaches decoupées*, not *papiers collés*: it is not a matter of taking a piece of paper, as the Cubists or the Dadaists did, and putting it into a composition, either drawn or painted, in order to emphasise the spatial gradations, in all their subtlety, through the object's direct or potential physical presence. Matisse's painted papers live imaginatively in a process that is technically and inventively quite different from painting because, by being used instead of paint, cut out and glued to the background, they become a form in themselves, and achieve results similar to those of painting. Indeed, they are able to generate spatial values, just as happens in a painting, directly, without other objects being involved.

There was no essential break between the oil paintings and the *gouaches decoupées*, as Matisse himself said in 1952. Matisse still had his old mental lucidity and his joy in creation, and these produced motifs with reduced, simplified forms, the colour of which was something necessary, irrevocable, and inherent in them. In 1952 he wrote: 'I have arrived at a form which achieves what is essential by keeping the line, the sign, of the object; at other times I have shown the object in its own complex space, but the sign is enough, is all that is needed to allow it to exist in the form that belongs to it, and in the surroundings for which I conceived it.'

In other words, there was no break: nothing came between the idea and its realisation except a pair of scissors. 'Drawing with scissors, cutting the colour out alive,' Matisse said, 'reminds me of the way a sculptor cuts the material himself.' He thus produced solid forms in the flimsiest materials.

These forms recall the dazzling richness of a distant vision of objects, flowers, seaweed and shells: all images from an endless fund of memory, all, recomposed as Matisse cut his papers surely and perfectly, taking on a new quality, a kind of irrevocable, emblematic quality. Pure colours, counterpointing one another, make delightful abstracts, the forms are synthesised into purer, more concentrated patterns, and Matisse's ever open and accessible imagination seems to go beyond the limitations of immediate sensibility.

Thus the large figure of *Zulma* 1950 (Statens Museum fur Kunst, Copenhagen) is imperiously stretched across a luminous glow of colours, yellow, green, blue, ochre, vermilion. *Chinese fish* 1951 (private collection, Paris) has an enamelled brilliance in its abstract forms and rhythmical arrangement of colour. Some of the most exhilarating *gouaches* appeared in 1952: *Women and monkeys* (private collection, Paris); *The Negress* (Bayler collection, Basle) with its jewel-like vividness in the juxtaposed black and red; *The sadness of the king* (Musée d'Art Moderne, Paris) in which once again the intense black makes the colours seem to throb, intensely expressive as they are in the superbly abstract images.

Other famous *gouaches decoupées* from 1954 are *The swimming pool* (private collection, Paris), *The tresses* and *Blue nude* (Bayler collection, Basle). In this latter work, the contraction of the form, which in no way diminishes the curved, relaxed attitudes of the figures in their various tones of blue, is found in the subtle, fluid white spaces between them. Each of these seems to return to the fresh, airy memories of Polynesia which Matisse had retained so long and so vividly. *Memory of Oceania* 1953 (Museum of Modern Art, New York) transfigures reality into an abstract concentration of colours and light; so does *The snail* 1953 (Tate Gallery, London), in which eloquence is found in the circle of gradually altering colours.

Dancers and acrobats, flowers and masks, transform rather than deform images and objects, constantly reinventing them. Nothing is repeated except Matisse's fresh, fragrant cutting of the paper and his choice of colours; see, for instance *Acanthus* 1954 (private collection, Paris), in which the airy fronds flow out into space, suggesting their breathless vibrations. In his *gouaches decoupées* Matisse does not so much recreate the luxuriant nature of Tahiti as transpose it in the enchantment of his imagination, an imagination able to prolong for a lifetime the pleasurable 'longing for islands', that 'terrible luxury'.

Matisse and the ballet

By cutting out forms in pure flat colours, the volume of which was dictated by the demands of the outline, by using his taste for decoration intelligently, Matisse designed the scenery and costumes for Stravinsky's *Le Rossignol*, which Diaghilev had cut down to a single act in 1920. Against backgrounds of white and various tones of blue, he designed costumes of brilliant, blinding imaginativeness, like the one for the emperor, who unfolded his great red cloak like a fan.

This decorative splendour found a response in the contradictory refinement of taste at the time, into which Matisse's influence spread through his paintings, his drawings and his stage designs. At the Paris Exhibition in 1925, this taste had its 'cluttered shop-windows', but Veronesi detected there, 'among the new voices which are raised almost unheard in the clamour of "decoration" . . . a clean line descending straight through Matisse, Brancusi and Modigliani, through Iribe and Lepape, to the faces of the midinettes'.

After an interval of many years, Matisse again designed scenery and costumes, in 1939. This was for Shostakovitch's *Rouge et Noir*, performed by the Ballet Russe of Monte Carlo, with choreography by Massine. The scenery was boldly conceived in a harmony of colour and design. Beyond large arches, supported by columns, the background was of triangles in three colours, red, blue and black, an orchestral harmony that kept loyally to Matisse's concept of colour. 'The expressive aspect of colour imposes itself upon me in a purely instinctive way,' he said. Some years later, in 1948, Roland Petit asked him to design for the ballet *La femme et son ombre*, but for various reasons the plan came to nothing.

Unlike other painters of his generation, Matisse did not work much in the theatre, although the idea of the figure moving gracefully and rhythmically to music would seem to respond to the motif of the dance, a theme he often used.

A reasonable art

In everything he did, in everything he created with that kind of Olympic calm, that almost neo-classical refinement, Matisse drew upon all kinds of cultures, all sorts of varied influences from past and present. But he used them always in a very personal way, knowing that he must give 'new, fresh inspiration' to everything he used.

The apparent ease with which he invented and solved problems in fact was in no way easily acquired. 'One reaches a state of creation through conscientious work,' he said. 'Preparing to carry it out means nourishing the feeling one has about it with studies that have a sort of similarity to the painting, and then one can make the choice of elements. It is, in fact, these studies that allow the painter to free his unconscious.' In this operation, it is necessary to work out the function of colour and of the drawing. 'It is no use having a mere avalanche of colours,' Matisse wrote. 'Colour reaches its full potential for expression only when it is organised, that is, when it corresponds to the intensity of the artist's emotion.' For this reason, he continued: 'It is not possible to separate drawing and colour. Because colour is never applied by chance; from the moment in which limitations, and, even more, proportions are created, there is a division. It is here that the painter's creation and personality intervene. But the drawing counts a great deal as well. It is the expression of the painter's domination of his objects. When you know an object completely, you can enclose it in an external line, which will define it completely.' From the friction between feeling and seeking comes the final balance: 'But drawing and colour are only a suggestion,' Matisse wrote. 'Through illusion, they must make the person looking at the painting possess the things in it.'

As early as 1907 Apollinaire had said that 'the prerogative of Matisse's art is to be reasonable,' and a few years later Matisse himself said that his art

16 *The Virgin,* study for the chapel
at Vence
1948–49, charcoal and ink
$130 \times 236\frac{1}{4}$ in (330×620 cm)
private collection

was becoming barer and 'in spite of its ever-increasing simplicity, it [had] become more sumptuous'. A well-tempered experience in graphic work was part of it, necessary to achieve these results. 'The vertical is in my spirit,' Matisse wrote. 'It helps me to make the direction of the light exact, and in my quick sketches I never indicate, say, a curved branch in a landscape without noting its relationship with the vertical. My curves are never wild.'

There was no concession, then, to the sudden emotion, to the spontaneous impulse, either graphic or decorative. Always there was a first stage, in which he analysed the work, 'a kind of meditation' through which even the 'quick sketches' of the past few years finally appeared as revelations, as part of a clear formal order, a clear meditative intelligence, in the Cartesian sense of *clarté*.

Matisse's writings are always declarations or confessions. In them he never tries to judge others, never defines a theory of painting, but clarifies – for himself rather than his reader – the reasons for, the meaning of, his style. Some words recur frequently, and they are in fact the ones that tend to express his way of working most precisely.

In October 1941, he confessed to his friend André Rouveyre how much the conflict between his acute sensibility and his rigorous method of work tormented him. 'I am utterly shaken by it,' he said, 'yet I remember that my whole life has been spent in this way. A moment of desire, followed by a happy moment of revelation which allows me to do something that goes beyond all reason and leaves me unprepared for the next undertaking. And although I know it will always happen to me in this way, I try to hold on to Ariadne's thread, which, logically, should lead me to express myself . . .'

Sensation was tempered by the hard tenacity of his method, until the time when the colours which had moved him in his relationship with nature could be expressed in the sphere of sympathy and harmony which Matisse had established between himself and the objects around him, among which he lived. In them, therefore, he wished to make room for his 'feelings of tenderness, without the risk of suffering for it, as happens in life'. Where in the end, while he confirmed the balanced fervour of his spirit, he seemed vulnerable to the 'ardent, cunning and lively ingenuity' that Rouveyre had learnt to appreciate during their long years of close friendship: a hidden, secret vein of uneasiness which Matisse never showed in his paintings, where he wanted 'to be happy and to make others happy'.

This was continued until the end: the elegant ivy, the flaming acanthus, the brilliant poppies, all the foliage he invented once again in his memory, appear in spaces of crystalline candour (see, for instance, the 1953 mural in the Brody collection in Los Angeles). Somewhere in his room, until the very end, were any number of sketches for a *Rape of Europa*, long dreamed about, never realised.

This is all Matisse is!

Throughout his creative life, the fundamental characteristic of Matisse's painting consisted, as Apollinaire pointed out, in 'being reasonable'. But this reasonableness might 'be passionate or tender, and it expressed itself so purely that anyone could understand it'.

Being true to himself did not mean being immobile. On the contrary, it meant tirelessly seeking among the riches which his principles, and his methods of work, had already tried and tested, with a freedom and an autonomy of vision that time had sharpened, instead of disappointing. 'I have worked for years,' he might have cried, 'for people to say: this is all Matisse is!'

Argan called him 'the most limpidly classical painter of the century, the Gide of modern painting . . . a synthetic, global representation of the world, indeed of the universe, because every feeling, when it is authentic and really fills our life with itself, gives us the experience not merely of that one particular object, but of the universe as a whole.' If this is so, then clearly Matisse is extremely important for our century.

This has nothing to do with the century's history of art in its gossipy detail –the supposed rivalry between Matisse and Picasso, for instance, or Matisse's indignation at the development of Cubism, or the events or the artists of German Expressionism. Braque on the one hand seems to touch on apparent contradictions, and in a sense Matisse seems stricter, in his compositions, than Braque himself. Picasso, on the other hand, seems influenced by Matisse's line in some of his graphic works, and comes close to what Penrose has called 'Matisse's boldest inventions' with his splashes of flat and brilliant colour.

Taken as a whole, the painting of our time has noted Matisse's ascendancy, in particular because of his use of colour, and often with what Leymarie calls a 'submissiveness that actually seems like affection'. But quite apart from this half-understanding imitation, his painting has been revealing to quite a few artists: for instance, De Stael, especially as far as the value of line is concerned, and the interest aroused by his *gouaches decoupées*; or Rothko, whose paintings betray obvious links with those of Matisse, both in the way he studies the character of colours, and in his way of interpreting colour in space. Then, too, there is Hans Hofmann, who shows no sign of slackening his interest, and who has acted as a bridge between the painting of the Blaue Reiter group and Matisse and American culture.

But, quite apart from his quality as a painter and the autonomy of his vision, maintained as a conscious act of faith, Matisse's greatest contribution to art lies in the matchless lesson he gave of pure, fertile creativity, ever renewed through the clear intelligence with which he chose his methods of expression. This creativity, with classical serenity, avoids being touched or compromised by the world's affairs, and is turned thoughtfully, meditatively, towards its own acquired inner happiness.

2

3

4-5

6

8

11

14

16

18

21

22

23

24

25

26

28

34

36

37

38

39

41

Description of colour plates

1 *Reader*
1895, oil on canvas
Musée National d'Art Moderne, Paris

2 *Still-life against the light*
1899, oil on canvas, 29 × 36¾ in (74 × 93·5 cm)

3 *Road to Collioure*
1905, oil on canvas, 30 × 33½ in (46 × 55 cm)
private collection, Paris

4–5 *Interior at Collioure*
1905, oil on canvas, 35½ × 28¾ in (60 × 73 cm)
private collection, Zurich

6 *Blue nude, memory of Biskra*
1907, oil on canvas, 36¼ × 55 in (92 × 140 cm)
Cone collection, Museum of Art, Baltimore

7 *The bluff*
1907, oil on canvas, 30¾ × 33½ in (73 × 60 cm)
Öffentliche Kunstsammlung, Basle

8 *Woman combing her hair*
1907, oil on canvas, 45¾ × 35 in (116 × 89 cm)
Staatsgalerie, Stockholm

9 *Seated nude*
1909, oil on canvas, 13 × 16 in (33 × 41 cm)
Musée de Peinture et de Sculpture, Grenoble

10 *Algerian woman*
1909, oil on canvas, 31½ × 25½ in (80 × 65 cm)
Musée National d'Art Moderne, Paris

11 *The Seine at Paris*
1911, oil on canvas
Marlborough Gallery, London

12–13 *Interior with aubergines*
1911, oil on canvas, 82½ × 96½ in (210 × 245 cm)
Musée de Peinture et de Sculpture, Grenoble

14 *Madame Matisse with a Manila shawl*
1911, oil on canvas, 44 × 27¼ in (112 × 69 cm)
Öffentliche Kunstsammlung, Basle

15 *Interior, fish in bowl*
1914, oil on canvas, 57¾ × 38¼ in (146·5 × 97·5 cm)
Musée National d'Art Moderne, Paris

16 *The window*
1916, oil on canvas, 57½ × 45½ in (146 × 116 cm)
Institute of Arts, Detroit

17 *Painter and model*
1917, oil on canvas, 57½ × 38 in (147 × 97 cm)
Musée National d'Art Moderne, Paris

18 *Sunshine*
1917, oil on canvas, 35¾ × 29 in (91 × 74 cm)
private collection, Paris

19 *Nude, Spanish carpet*
1919, oil on canvas, 25 × 21¼ in (64 × 54 cm)
private collection, Paris

20 *Woman with an umbrella*
1919, oil on canvas, 25½ × 18 in (65 × 46 cm)
Silvan Kocher collection, Solothurn

21 *Seated woman*
1919, oil on canvas, 22 × 15½ in (56 × 39 cm)
Gianni Mattioli collection, Milan

22 *Seated woman*
1919–20, oil on canvas
Galleria Marlborough, Rome

23 *Woman on a sofa*
1920, oil on canvas, 23½ × 28¾ in (60 × 73 cm)
Öffentliche Kunstsammlung, Basle

24 *Fishes*
1921, oil on canvas
Thompson collection, Pittsburgh

25 *Odalisque with red trousers*
1922, oil on canvas
Musée National d'Art Moderne, Paris

26 *Seated nude with red background*
1925, oil on canvas, 17 × 23½ in (43 × × 60 cm)
Musée National d'Art Moderne, Paris

27 *Seated nude with drum*
1926, oil on canvas, 28¾ × 23¼ in (73 × 54 cm)
William S. Paley collection, New York

28 *The buffet*
1928, oil on canvas, 32¼ × 39½ in (82 × 100 cm)
Musée National d'Art Moderne, Paris

29 *Loulou*
1929, oil on canvas
Thompson collection, Pittsburgh

30–31 *Pink nude*
1935, oil on canvas, 23½ × 36¼ in (60 × 92 cm)
Cone collection, Museum of Art, Baltimore

32 *Hungarian in a green blouse*
1939, oil on canvas
Jan Salomon collection, Geneva

33 *The Rumanian blouse*
1940, oil on canvas, 36¼ × 28½ in (92 × 72 cm)
Musée National d'Art Moderne, Paris

34 *Still-life with oysters*
1940, oil on canvas, 25½ × 31¾ in (65 × 81 cm)
Öffentliche Kunstsammlung, Basle

35 *Girl in pink*
1942, oil on canvas
Thompson collection, Pittsburgh

36 *Still-life with lemons*
1943, oil on canvas
Thompson collection, Pittsburgh

37 *Red interior*
1947, oil on canvas
Kunstnordrhein, Westphalia

38 *The swimmer in the aquarium*
1947, lithograph for the book *Jazz*

39 *The Codomas*
1947, lithograph for the book *Jazz*

40 *Large red interior*
1948, oil on canvas, 45½ × 35 in (116 × 89 cm)
Musée National d'Art Moderne, Paris

41 *Seated nude*
bronze
Musée National d'Art Moderne, Paris

Biographical outline

1869. Henri Matisse is born December 31st at Le Cateau-Cambrésis in northern France, to Émile Matisse, corn-merchant, and his wife Anna Gérand. His childhood is spent at his parents' home in rue de la République.

1887–88. He leaves the secondary school in St Quentin and studies at the Faculty of Law in Paris.

1889. He works in a lawyer's office in St Quentin.

1890. He begins to paint during a long convalescence after an operation; his mother had given him a box of paints. He takes courses in drawing at the Ecole Quentin de la Tour, although he still keeps his job, and decorates his grandparents' house at Le Cateau-Cambrésis.

1891. He overcomes his father's opposition, gives up his job, and moves to Paris to study painting. At the Académie Julian he studies under Bouguereau.

1892. He goes to evening classes at the Ecole des Arts Décoratifs, where he meets Albert Marquet.

1894. His daughter Marguerite is born; he is to marry her mother, Amélie Parayre, in 1898.

1895. He leaves the Académie Julian. Gustave Moreau notices him and takes him into his *atelier* at the Ecole des Beaux-Arts, excusing him the entrance exam. Here he meets Rouault, Manguin, Camoin, Flandrin, Evenepoel and other young pupils. At the Louvre he copies many old masters, particularly the French (Poussin, Watteau, Chardin) and Dutch (Van der Heyden, de Heem). He has a studio at 19 quai St Michel, next door to Emile Wéry's. In summer, his first stay in Brittany.

1896. He exhibits for the first time at the Salon of the Société Nationale des Beaux-Arts. *The woman reading* was bought by the State for the president's residence. Summer stay in Brittany, at Belle-Ile, where he meets John Russell, a friend of the Impressionists, who introduces him to Pissarro and Rodin.

1897. He exhibits again at the Salon de la Société Nationale. Spends summer at Belle-Ile again.

1898. He marries Amélie Parayre. Journey to London to study Turner. Long stay in Corsica and near Toulouse.

1899. He exhibits for the last time at the Salon de la Société Nationale. Cormon takes over from Moreau, who had died, at the Ecole des Beaux-Arts, so Matisse moves to the Académie Carrière, where he meets Derain and Puy. He goes to evening classes at the school of sculpture in the rue Etienne-Marcel, buys Cézanne's *Three bathers*, Gauguin's *Head of a boy* and a plaster cast by Rodin, and reads Signac's *From Eugène Delacroix to Neo-Impressionism*. His son Jean is born.

1900. Financial troubles. His wife opens a dress shop in the rue de Chateaudun. He works with Marquet on decorations for the Grand Palais. His son Pierre is born.

1901. He exhibits for the first time at the Salon des Indépendants, of which Signac is president. At the retrospective exhibition of Van Gogh, Derain introduced him to Vlaminck ('I was touched to find ideas so similar to my own in these youngsters'). The critic Roger-Marx introduces him to the gallery-owner Berthe Weill. A rest cure in Switzerland after bronchitis.

1902. He begins to exhibit at the Weill Gallery, and spends the winter with his parents at Bohain.

1903. The Autumn Salon is set up and he begins to exhibit there regularly. He makes his first etchings.

1904. Exhibition at Vollards', presented by Roger-Marx. Summer stay at St Tropez, with Signac and Cross.

1905. *Luxe, calme et volupté* shown at the Salon des Indépendants, bought by Signac. Summer at Collioure with Derain; he meets Maillol and Daniel de Monfreid. He exhibits at the Autumn Salon with Derain, Manguin, Marquet, Valtat, Vlaminck, Weiss and Rouault, 'la cage des fauves'. First purchase by the Steins; he begins visiting their home, where he is to meet Picasso.

1906. He exhibits *Bonheur de vivre* at the Salon des Indépendants, and takes part in the Autumn Salon with the other Fauves. One-man show at Druet's. First short stay in Algeria, at Biskra. He spends the summer at Collioure and makes his first lithographs and woodcuts.

1907. Journey to Italy: Padua, Florence, Arezzo, Siena. At the Autumn Salon he shows *Le Luxe*.

1908. On the advice of Sarah Stein and Hans Purmann he opens an *atelier*, particularly for foreigners, first in the rue de Sèvres, then at 33 Boulevard des Invalides. He spends the summer in Bavaria. First exhibitions abroad: in New York, Moscow and Berlin. He publishes 'Notes d'un peintre' in the 25th December number of *La Grande Revue*.

1909. First contract with Bernheim-Jeune. He spends the summer at Cavaliere. Although he keeps a studio in Paris, he sets up home at Issy-les-Moulineaux, on the road to Camart. Shchukin, the Russian collector, commissions two large panels.

1910. With Marquet, he visits the exhibition of Islamic art in Munich. At the Autumn Salon, he exhibits *The dance* and *Music*, Shchukin's panels. He spends the winter in Andalusia.

1911. Journey to Moscow, to set up Shchukin's panels; there, he is interested by Russian icons. He works mostly at Issy-les-Moulineaux and spends the summer at Collioure.

1912. A long stay in Tangiers with Marquet and Camoin. First exhibition of sculpture in New York.

1913. In April he exhibits sculpture and paintings from Morocco at Bernheim-Jeune's. He takes part in the Sezession in Berlin and at the Armory Show in New York.

1914. He has an atelier in Paris, at 19 quai St Michel. After the outbreak of war he moves to Collioure, where he meets Juan Gris, with his family.

1917. He spends the summer with Marquet at Chenonceaux, and at the beginning of winter joins him again at Marseilles. During his convalescence from an illness he moves to Nice, where he lives at the Hôtel Beau-Rivage. New contract with Bernheim-Jeune.

1918. He lives at Nice, at the Hôtel de la Mediterranée, and often visits Renoir at Cagnes.

1919. Exhibitions in Paris and London.

1920. Designs scenery and costumes for Stravinsky's *Le Rossignol*, for Diaghilev's Russian ballet. He spends the summer in London and then at Etretat.

1921. Another stay at Etretat. He spends most of the year at Nice, in the place Charles-Félix.

1923. Matisse's forty-eight paintings and two drawings belonging to the Russian collectors Morosov and Shchukin confiscated after the October Revolution, and put into the Museum of Modern Western Art in Moscow.

1924. Exhibitions in New York and Copenhagen.

1925. Another journey to Italy.

1927. He wins the Carnegie prize for painting, in Pittsburgh.

1930. Journey to Polynesia; stay in Tahiti. In the autumn goes to Pittsburgh as a member of the jury for the Carnegie prize. Albert Barnes commissions a mural decoration (*The dance*) for the central hall of the Barnes Foundation in Merion.

1931. At Nice, he works on the painting for Barnes. He makes the illustrations for Mallarmé's *Poésies*.

1932. Second and definitive version of *The dance* for Barnes.

1933. Journey to the United States, to set up *The dance* in Merion. On his return to Europe he lands in Venice and spends some time in the vicinity.

1934. His son, Pierre Matisse, organises a series of exhibitions at his gallery in New York.

1935. He makes a cartoon for a tapestry for Marie Cuttoli.

1936. He illustrates an American edition of James Joyce's *Ulysses* with etchings.

1938. He stays at the Hôtel Regina at Cimiez, near Nice. Scenery and costumes for Shostakovitch's *Rouge et Noir* for the Ballet Russe of Monte Carlo, performed in the spring of 1939.

1940. After the fall of France, he considers going to Brazil; then gives up the idea and settles in Nice again.

1941. At Lyons he has a serious operation. He begins to illustrate Ronsard's *Florilège des Amours*.

1943. As the situation worsens in France he moves to Vence, to the villa *Le Rêve*, where he lives until 1948.

17 *Self-portrait* 1904
Metropolitan Museum of Art,
New York

18 *Portrait of Matisse* by André
Derain, 1905
Tate Gallery, London

19 *Self-portrait* 1906
Statens Museum fur Kunst,
Copenhagen

20 Photograph of Matisse, Camoin
and Marquet

1944. He works on *gouaches decoupées* and *papiers collés* to illustrate *Jazz* (with a text of poetry, also by Matisse, published by Tériade in 1947).

1945. Retrospective exhibition in the Hall of Honour at the Autumn Salon. Exhibition in London, with Picasso.

1946. He makes the cartoons for *Polynesia*, later woven at Beauvais in 1949.

1947. He is given the Legion of Honour.

1948. He works almost entirely on the Chapel of the Rosary of the Dominican convent in Vence. Retrospective exhibition at the Philadelphia Museum.

1949. He moves to the Hôtel Regina in Nice, where he celebrates his 80th birthday.

1950. One-man show at the 25th Biennale in Venice; he receives the Gran Premio for a non-Italian artist.

1951. On June 25th, the Chapel of the Rosary in Vence is opened.

1952. At Le Cateau-Cambrésis a small museum named after Matisse is opened.

1954. Matisse dies on November 3rd and is buried in the small cemetery at Cimiez, in a spot presented by the city of Nice.

Main exhibitions

1896. Salon of the Société Nationale des Beaux-Arts, Paris.

1897. Exhibits *La Desserte* at the Salon of the Société Nationale des Beaux-Arts, Paris.

1899. Salon of the Société Nationale des Beaux-Arts, Paris.

1901. Salon des Indépendants, Paris.

1903. First Salon d'Automne, Paris.

1904. June: first one-man show at Vollard's, Paris (catalogue introduction by Roger-Marx).

1905. Salon des Indépendants, Paris, and the Salon d'Automne, Paris.

1906. Exhibits *Bonheur de vivre* at the Salon des Indépendants, Paris. Salon d'Automne. One-man show at the Gallery Druet, Paris.

1907. Salon d'Automne, Paris.

1908. One-man show at Gallery 291, New York. One-man show at the Gallery of the Golden Fleece, Moscow. One-man show at the Gallery Cassirer in Berlin.

1910. One-man show at the Gallery Bernheim-Jeune, Paris. Salon d'Automne, Paris.

1912. One-man show of sculpture at the Gallery 291, New York.

1913. April: paintings and sculpture at the Gallery Bernheim-Jeune, Paris. Sezession, Berlin and the Armory Show, New York, Chicago and Boston.

1914. One-man shows at the Gerlit Gallery, Berlin and the Montrose Gallery, New York.

1918. January: exhibits with Picasso at the Gallery Paul Guillaume, Paris (catalogue introduction by Apollinaire).

1919. One-man show at the Gallery Bernheim-Jeune, Paris, and the Leicester Galleries, London.

1920. One-man show at the Gallery Bernheim-Jeune, Paris.

1921. Carnegie exhibition, Pittsburgh.

1922. One-man show at the Gallery Bernheim-Jeune, Paris.

1923. One-man show at the Gallery Bernheim-Jeune, Paris.

1924. One-man shows at the Brunner Gallery, New York, and the Gallery Bernheim-Jeune, Paris. Ny Carlsberg Glyptotek, Copenhagen (catalogue introduction by L. S. Swane). Carnegie exhibition, Pittsburgh.

1925. Carnegie exhibition, Pittsburgh.

1926. Carnegie exhibition, Pittsburgh.

1927. One-man shows at the Gallery Bernheim-Jeune, Paris, and the Dudening Gallery, New York. He exhibits in the Carnegie exhibition, Pittsburgh, and wins first prize.

1928. One-man show at the Valentine Gallery, New York.

1929. One-man show at the Gallery Bernheim-Jeune, Paris.

1930. One-man show at the Gallery Thannhauser, Berlin.

1931. One-man show at the Gallery Georges Petit, Paris. Kunsthalle, Basle. Museum of Modern Art, New York (catalogue introduction by Alfred H. Barr).

1932. Original etchings to illustrate Mallarmé's *Poésies* at the Gallery Marie Narriman, New York.

1934. First exhibition of a series organised by the Gallery Pierre Matisse, New York: paintings.

1936. One-man show at the Gallery Paul Rosenberg, Paris. Gallery Pierre Matisse New York: studies for Shchukin's *The dance*.

1937. One room at the exhibition *Maîtres de l'art indépendant* at the Petit Palais, Paris.

1938. Gallery Pierre Matisse, New York: paintings and drawings. Exhibits with Picasso and Braque in Oslo, Copenhagen and Stockholm.

1941. Recent drawings at the Gallery Louis Carré, Paris.

1943. One-man show at the Gallery Pierre Matisse, New York.

1945. Retrospective exhibition in the Hall of Honour at the Salon d'Automne. Exhibits with Picasso at the Victoria and Albert Museum, London (preface by C. Zervos), then at the Palais des Beaux-Arts, Brussels. Gallery Pierre Matisse, New York: drawings.

1948. Retrospective exhibition at the Museum of Art, Philadelphia.

1949. Gallery Pierre Matisse, New York: recent drawings. Musée National d'Art

Moderne, Paris (catalogue introduction by J. Cassou). Large retrospective exhibition (308 works) at the Kunsthalle, Lucerne.

1950. Gallerie des Ponchettes, Nice (catalogue introduction by G. Salles). Maison de la Pensée française, Paris (catalogue introduction by Aragon). One room at the 25th Biennale Internazionale d'Arte, Venice. Palazzo Barberini, Ente Premi Roma, Rome (catalogue introduction by R. Cogniat).

1951. Museum of Art, New York, and the Museums of Cleveland, Chicago and San Francisco. Retrospective exhibition at the National Museum, Tokyo.

1952. The Berggruen Gallery organises a series of exhibitions of which the first is of recent engravings; others followed of *gouaches decoupées* (1953), rare lithographs (1954), and unpublished drawings and sculptures (1958).

1956. Retrospective exhibition at the Musée National d'Art Moderne, Paris (catalogue introduction by J. Cassou).

1958. Gallery Bernheim-Dauberville, Paris (catalogue introduction by J. & H. Dauberville).

1959. *Gouaches decoupées* at the Kunsthalle, Berne (catalogue introduction by F. Meyer).

1966. *Matisse und seine freunde*, at the Kunstverein, Hamburg (catalogue introduction by H. Platt).

1968. Retrospective exhibition at the Hayward Gallery, London (catalogue introduction by Lawrence Gowing).

1969. Retrospective exhibition at The Hermitage, Leningrad.

1970. A large exhibition at the Grand Palais, Paris.

Bibliography

MAIN BOOKS ILLUSTRATED BY MATISSE

PIERRE REVERDY, *Les jockeys camouflés*, Paris, 1918 (with 5 drawings); STEPHANE MALLARMÉ, *Poésies*, Skira, Lausanne, 1932 (with 29 original etchings); JAMES JOYCE, *Ulysses*, Macy, New York, 1935 (with 6 original etchings); TRISTAN TZARA, *Midis gagnés*, Denoël, Paris, 1939 (with 6 drawings); HENRI DE MONTHERLANT, *Pasiphäe, Chant de Minos*, Fabiani Éditeur, Paris, 1944 (with 18 original engravings); PIERRE REVERDY, *Visages, poésies*, Les Éditions du Chêne, Paris, 1946 (with 14 lithographs); ANDRÉ ROUVEYRE, *Repli*, Paris, 1947 (with 12 lithographs); CHARLES BAUDELAIRE, *Les fleurs du mal*, Paris, 1947 (with 1 etching, 69 woodcuts and 33 photo-lithographs); HENRI MATISSE, *Jazz*, Éditions Verve, Paris, 1947 (with 20 lithographs); *Florilège des Amours de Ronsard*, Paris, 1948 (with 127 lithographs).

MATISSE'S WRITINGS

'Notes d'un peintre', *La Grande Revue*, 25 December, 1908; 'Notes autobiographiques', *Formes*, Paris, January 1930; 'On Modernism and Tradition', *The Studio*, London, 9 May, 1935; 'Divagations', *Verve* no. 1, December 1937; 'Notes d'un peintre sur son dessin', *Le Point*, special number, July 1939; 'Observations on Painting', *Horizon*, London, 7 March, 1946; 'Comment j'ai fait mes livres', *Anthologie du livre illustré*, Skira, Geneva, 1946; 'Le Chemin de la couleur', *Art présent*, Paris, 1947; *Jazz*, Paris, 1947; 'L'exactitude n'est pas la verité', catalogue of the A.P.I.A.W. exhibition of drawings, Liège, 1948; 'Henri Matisse parle', *Praits*, no. 8, March 1950; 'La Chapelle du Rosaire des Domenicaines à Vence', preface by Henri Matisse, Vence, 1951; 'Message à sa ville natale', 8 November, 1952, in the catalogue of the Henri Matisse museum at Le Cateau-Cambrésis.

MONOGRAPHS AND GENERAL BOOKS

(N.B. for complete biographical documentation see, A. H. Barr Jr., *Matisse and his public*, New York, 1951, up to that date; for the following years, see in particular the biographical notes in the catalogue of the exhibition held in Paris in 1970).

M. SEMBAT, *Henri Matisse*, Paris, 1920; CHARLES VILDRAC, *Cinquante dessins d'Henri Matisse*, Paris, 1920; R. SCHACHT, *Henri Matisse*, Dresden, 1922; A. BASLER, *Henri Matisse*, Leipzig, 1924; W. GEORGE, *Dessins d'Henri Matisse*, Paris, 1925; F. FELS, *Henri Matisse*, Paris, 1929; A. BERTRAM, *Matisse*, London and New York, 1930; ROGER FRY, *Matisse*, New York, 1930; G. JEDLICKA, *Henri Matisse*, Paris, 1930; A. BARNES and V. DE MAZIA, *The art of Henri Matisse*, New York, 1933; P. COURTHION, *Henri Matisse*, Paris, 1934; R. KAWASHIMA, *Matisse*, Tokyo, 1934; R. ESCHOLIER, *Matisse*, Paris, 1937; A. ROMM, *Matisse*, Leningrad, 1937; C. ROGER-MARX, *Dessins d'Henri Matisse*, Paris, 1939; J. CASSOU, *Matisse*, Paris, 1939 (second edition, 1947); G. TESTORI, *Henri Matisse, disegni*, Milan, 1943; G. BESSON, *Matisse*, Paris, 1943; P. COURTHION, *Le visage de Matisse*, Lausanne, 1943; L. SWANE, *Henri Matisse*, Stockholm, 1944; I. GRUNEWALD, *Matisse och expressionismen*, Stockholm, 1944; M. VALSECCHI, *Disegni di Matisse*, Milan, 1944; B. DORIVAL, *Le Fauvisme et le Cubisme*, Paris, 1944; LOUIS ARAGON, *Matisse*, Geneva, 1946; G. SCHIEWILLER, *Matisse*, Milan, 1947; J. LEJARD, *Matisse*, Paris, 1948; M. MALINGUE, *Matisse, Dessins*, Paris, 1949; G. DUTHUIT, *Les Fauves*, Geneva, 1949; A. H. BARR, JR., *Matisse and his public*, New York, 1951; G. DIEHL, *Matisse*, Paris, 1951; J. REWALD, *Les Fauves*, New York, 1952 (catalogue of the exhibition at the Museum of Modern Art, New York); C. GREENBERG, *Henri Matisse*, New York, 1953; J. JEDLICKA, *Die Matisse-Kapelle in Vence*, Frankfurt, 1955; M. GEORGES-MICHEL, *De Renoir à Picasso*, Paris, 1955; R. ESCHOLIER, *Matisse ce vivant*, Paris, 1956; J.-J. MULLER, *Le Fauvisme*, Paris, 1956; A. SALMON, *Le Fauvisme*, Paris, 1956; C. ZERVOS, *Histoire de l'art contemporain*, Paris, 1958; J. LASSAIGNE, *Matisse*, Geneva, 1959; U. APOLLONIO, *Fauves e Arbisti*, Bergamo, 1959; J. LEYMARIE, *Le Fauvisme*, Geneva, 1959; J.-P. CRESPELLE, *I Fauves*, Florence, 1962; J. SELZ, *Matisse*, Milan, 1964; G. MARCHIORI, *Matisse, son oeuvre, son universe*, Paris, 1967; M. LUZI and M. CARRÀ, *L'opera di Matisse dalla rivolta 'fauve' all'intimismo, 1904–28*, Rizzoli.

MAIN SPECIAL NUMBERS OF REVIEWS CONCERNING MATISSE

Les Cahiers d'aujourd'hui, Crès, Paris, 1921 (text by E. FAURE, J. ROMAINS, C. VILDRAC and L. WERTH); *Cahiers d'art*, Paris, 1931 (text by P. FIERENS, P. GUEGUEN, G. SALLES, R. FRY, H. MCBRIDE, W. GROHMANN, C. ZERVOS, G. SCHEIWILLER, G. APOLLINAIRE); *Chroniques du Jour*, Paris, April 1931 (text by A. LHOTE, W. GEORGE, G. ROUAULT, F. FELS, A. LEVINSON, R. FRY, F. NEUGASS, R. REY, P. FIERENS, C. ROGER-MARX, G. APOLLINAIRE, C. ZERVOS, L. VAUXCELLES, M. SEMBAT, J. ROMAINS, B. TERNOVETS); *Le Point*, Lanzac, July 1939 (text by MATISSE, R. HUYGHE, J. PUY, G. BESSON, R. COGNIAT); *Verve*, no. 13, November 1945 (text by TÉRIADE and ROUVEYRE); *Art présent*, no. 2, 1947 (text by MATISSE, F. ELGAR, PIGNON, J. CASSOU, G. POULAIN); *Yomiuri*, Tokyo, 1951; *Art News Annual*, no. 21, New York, 1951 (text by G. SALLES and TÉRIADE); *La Biennale di Venezia*, no. 26, 1955 (text by MATISSE, P. MARTIN, B. BERENSON, M. GEORGES-MICHEL, S. BRANZI, S. BETTINI, C. BRANDI, G. MARCHIORI, G. C. ARGAN, F. RUSSOLI, P. MATISSE, P. MICHAUT); *Verve*, no. 35–36, Paris, 1958 (text by P. REVERDY and G. DUTHUIT).

MAIN ARTICLES IN REVIEWS

L. VAUXCELLES, *Gil Blas*, 14 October, 1904; A. GIDE, 'Promenade au Salon d'Automne', *Gazette des Beaux-Arts*, 1905, XLVII; G. APOLLINAIRE, *La Phalange*, 15 January, 1907; B. BERENSON, 'Letter to the Editor', *The Nation*, 12 November, 1908; ESTIENNE, *Les Nouvelles*, 12 April, 1909; G. APOLLINAIRE, *L'Intransigéant*, 18 March, 1901; G. STEIN, 'Henri Matisse-Pablo Picasso', *Camera Work*, August 1912; M. SEMBAT, *Les Cahiers d'aujourd'hui*, April 1913; F. TUGENDHOLD, 'The French Collection of S.I. Shchukin', *Apollo*, no. 1–2, 1914; W. PACH, 'Why Matisse?', *Century Magazine*, 6 February, 1915; M. and A. LEBLOND, *La Vie*, January 1918; R. SWAB, *L'amour de l'art*, October, 1920; H. PURRMANN, 'Uber Matisse', *Genius*, 1920; L. SWANE, 'Matisse i Tetzen Lunds samling', *Tilskuren*, 16 September, 1922; F. FELS, 'Propos d'artiste, Henri Matisse', *Les Nouvelles Littéraires*, 5 January, 1925; F. WATSON, *The Arts*, January 1927; M. TOZZI, 'Rouault e Matisse', *Le Arti Plastiche*, 16 November, 1927; E. TÉRIADE, 'Visite à Matisse', *L'Intransigéant*, 14 and 22 January, 1929; A. LEVINSON, 'Les soixante ans de Matisse', *L'Art vivant*, 1 January, 1930; R. HUYGHE, 'Matisse et la couleur', *Formes*, January 1930; F. NEUGASS, *Die Kunst*, October 1929 and *Cahiers de Belgique*, March, 1930; M. BERTELLO PANCERA, 'Note sull'arte di Matisse', *L'Arte*, no. 5, 1930; G. POULAIN, 'Sculptures d'Henri Matisse', *Formes*, November 1930; W. GEORGE, 'The double aspect of Matisse', *Formes*, June 1931; P. COURTHION, 'Rencontre avec Matisse', *Les Nouvelles Littéraires*, 27 June, 1931; MEYER-SCHAPIRO, 'Matisse und Impressionism', *Androcles*, February 1932; C. ROGER-MARX, 'L'oeuvre grave d'Henri Matisse', *Arts et Métiers Graphiques*, 15 March, 1933; L. GILLET, 'La Danse d'Henri Matisse à Merion', *Beaux-Arts*, 26 May, 1933; G. DUTHUIT, 'The Vitality of Henri Matisse', *The Listener*, 19 February, 1936; E. TÉRIADE, *Minotaure*, 15 October, 1936; H. DE MONTHERLANT, 'En écoutant Matisse', *L'Art et les Artistes*, July 1938; P. FIERENS, *Emporium*, October 1938; P. GUEGUEN, 'Les sculptures d'un grand peintre', *XX siècle*, December, 1938; L. GILLET, 'Une visite à Henri Matisse', *Candide*, 24 February, 1943; F. CARCO, 'Souvenir d'atelier', *Die Kunst Zeitung*, August 1943; G. DIEHL, 'Conversations avec Henri Matisse', *Les Arts et les Lettres*, 19 April, 1946; G. DIEHL, 'La Chapelle de Vence' *Les Amis de l'Art*, 1 October, 1948; P. BUCARELLI, 'I Fauves et Matisse', *Ulisse*, June 1950; A. H. BARR JR., 'Matisse, Picasso and the crisis of 1907', *Magazine of Art*, May 1951; DANIEL-ROPS, 'L'acte de foi de Matisse', *Le Journal de Genève*, 22 September, 1951; A. LEJARD, *Les Amis de l'Art*, October 1951; J. T. SOBY, 'Matisse from a psycho-analytical point of view', *College Art Journal*, XX, 1952–53; B. CHAMPIGNEUILLE, 'Mort du "Grand Fauve" ', *France Illustration*, no. 418, January 1955; A. ROUVEYRE, 'Matisse évoqué', *Revue des Arts*, June 1956; W. S. LIEBERMANN, 'Henri Matisse', *Print*, August 1956; G. DUTHUIT, 'Material and spiritual worlds of Henri Matisse', *Art News*, October 1956; R. ESCHOLIER, 'D'où vient Matisse?' *Prisme des Arts*, no. 4, 1956; L. DEGAND, 'Pour une revision des valeurs: Matisse, un génie?', *Aujourd'hui*, II, 1956; J. LEYMARIE, 'Le jardin du Paradis', *Lettres Françaises*, 6 August, 1959; J. LASSAIGNE, 'La peinture sans limites', *Lettres Françaises*, 6 August, 1959; E. HUTTINGER, 'Henri Matisse scultore', *Arte figurativa antica e moderna*, no. 4, 1959; G. L. LUZZATTO, 'Il guidizio di Hans Purrmann sui maestri francesi', *Commentari*, no. 1–2, 1960; R. BERNIER, 'Le Musée Matisse à Nice', *L'Oeil*, no. 105, 1963; F. ANDERSON TRAPP, 'Art Nouveau aspects of early Matisse', *Art Journal*, no. 1, 1966; C. GREENBERG, 'Matisse in 1966', *Boston Museum Bulletin*, no. 336, 1966; H. KRAMER, 'Matisse as a sculptor', *Boston Museum Bulletin*, no. 336; H. J. SELDIS, 'The magic of Matisse', *Apollo*, no. 50, 1966; J.-J. LEVEQUE, 'Matisse', *Le Arti*, no. 7–8, 1967; J. THIRION, 'L'enrichissement des collections modernes de 1958 à 1963, Musée de Nice', *La Revue du Louvre et des Musées de France*, no. 1, 1967; A. FORGE, A. HODKIN, P. KING, 'The relevance of Matisse', *Studio International*, no. 902, 1968; H. COULONGES, 'Matisse et le Paradis', *Connaissance des Arts*, no. 214, 1969; A. HILTON, 'Matisse in Moscow', *Art Journal*, no. 2, 1969–70; W. TUCKER, 'The sculpture of Matisse', *Studio International*, no. 913, 1969; W. TUCKER, 'Four sculptors. Part 3: Matisse', *Studio International*, no. 925, 1970; P. SCHNEIDER, 'Henri Matisse', *Revue du Louvre*, no. 2, 1970; F. WOIMANT, 'Matisse graveur et peintre du livre', no. 2, 1970; D. SUTTON, 'The Mozart of painting', *Apollo*, no. 105, 1970; M. GUIY, 'Matisse et la naissance du Fauvisme', *Gazette des Beaux-Arts*, May–June, 1970.